Praise for *Love as a Business Strategy*

"*Love as a Business Strategy* is a must-read for anyone embarking on the path to create Loving Organizations! Mohammad's gripping first-person perspective is so open, vulnerable, and touching. His journey to becoming a loving leader will inspire everyone to dig deeper within themselves to ask themselves 'Do I love my people? Do I love my organization?' The answer may be unsettling as it was for Mohammad and the leaders of Softway, which is exactly what is needed for each of us to embark on our own transformational journeys. I am truly grateful that my colleague recommended this book to me; it is definitely on my list of top organizational culture change books to read!"

"Our Loving Organization Consortium in collaboration with Compassion Café held a book club around *Love as a Business Strategy*. We were fortunate that Mohammad himself was able to attend, and shared incredibly profound insights about the degree of courage and humility, self-forgiveness. and compassion that he had to gather in the course of becoming an incredibly loving leader, as well as the nuanced interchange between personal and organizational transformation."

—Dr. Apurv Gupta
Vice President of Business
Development, Premier Inc.

"*Love as a Business Strategy* provides a brutally honest yet inspiring roadmap for transforming higher education institutions into cultures of care where every student is supported to achieve their goals. By connecting with students as whole human beings and addressing the challenges they face, *Love as a Business Strategy* compellingly argues colleges can boost completion rates while cultivating change makers. As an administrator seeking to serve all students, I found practical strategies and motivation in the book to call to dismantle inequitable systems and lead with empathy, understanding. and commitment to student success."

—Dr. Frances Villagran-Glover
President, Houston Community
College-Southeast

"The real-life examples documented in *Love as a Business Strategy* teach the incredible value of introspection and make this book a transformative guide for healthcare leaders. The principles shared within this book prove to us the power of compassion and empathy in both patient care and employee relationships. By embracing love as a strategic cornerstone, we can elevate the experiences of those we serve and foster a culture of kindness and support within our healthcare teams."

—Nick Marsico
President and CEO, Magruder Hospital

"*Love as a Business Strategy* is needed now more than ever. Positive changes to culture and organizations will change lives, and this book gives you a roadmap on how to do it. We need to change the narrative that success in business can't come with love and compassion. In fact, it is necessary. With many examples, insights, and practical tools, this is the book for the leaders of our organizations."

—Judy Le
CEO, TakeRoot Leadership Consulting

"*Love as a Business Strategy* is a critical read for any team and business leader interested in establishing a resilient culture built on trust, accountability, and empathy for all."

—Jeff Mechlem
Principal, Managing Director, Page

"*Love as a Business Strategy* completely changed the way we approach leadership and culture in our company. A totally honest and vulnerable account of how Love can lead to real success."

—Robert Gondo
Director, Tokyo Gardens Catering

"As a career public school educator, principal, and now superintendent of schools, I never suspected I would find the secret sauce to transforming school culture in a book titled *Love as a Business Strategy*. However, that is exactly what happened! Authors Mohammad, Chris, Frank, and Jeff led our leadership team of 40 on a journey of self-discovery toward a horizon of love for those we serve."

—Michael A. Amadei, Ed.D.
Superintendent of Schools,
Community Consolidated School District 62

"Organizations founded on greed, power, control, and self-centered shareholder-maximizing strategies have not served us well. We need responsible and humanistic organizations that focus on human dignity and societal well-being. In this book, through the case transformation of Softway, the authors show us a compelling way to centralize humanity in the workplace. *Love as a Business Strategy* is real and much needed to transform the way we organize and lead our organizations. Through their examples and practical tips, the authors weave a story of 'love in the workplace.' This transformation is possible! It can be done. *Love as a Business Strategy* shows us how. A must-read for all managers, leaders, and C-Suite executives!"

—Dr. Shaista Khilji
Professor of Human and
Organizational Learning at The George
Washington University

"*Love as a Business Strategy* elevates what it means (and takes) to create a truly successful company. This is a raw, honest book filled with practical insights and inspiring stories."

—Marc Effron
President of The Talent Strategy Group and Harvard Business Review *author*

"Love is wanting nothing but the best for another person. Love is more than feelings and emotion. Love is action. Love is a verb. And *Love as a Business Strategy* provides a proven approach with simple actions any organization can apply to maximize their future growth by empowering their people to become the best version of themselves."

—James Robert Lay
bestselling author of
Banking on Digital Growth *and CEO of*
the Digital Growth Institute

LOVE AS A BUSINESS STRATEGY

UPDATED EDITION

LOVE AS A BUSINESS STRATEGY

Resilience, Belonging & Success

UPDATED EDITION

MOHAMMAD F. ANWAR | FRANK E. DANNA
JEFFREY F. MA | CHRISTOPHER J. PITRE

WILEY

Published by John Wiley & Sons, Inc., Hoboken, New Jersey.
Published simultaneously in Canada.

For general information on our other products and services or for technical support, please contact our Customer Care Department within the United States at (800) 762-2974, outside the United States at (317) 572-3993 or fax (317) 572-4002.

Wiley also publishes its books in a variety of electronic formats. Some content that appears in print may not be available in electronic formats. For more information about Wiley products, visit our web site at www.wiley.com.

Library of Congress Cataloging-in-Publication Data is Available:

ISBN 9781394332533 (Cloth)
ISBN 9781394332557 (ePub)
ISBN 9781394332564 (ePDF)

Cover Design by Derek George
Author Photos: Courtesy of the Authors

SKY10094960_010225

To the past, present, and future employees and customers of Softway.

Contents

Foreword

When you first hear the title *Love as a Business Strategy*, you might feel skeptical. Believe me, I get it. Love doesn't often fit into spreadsheets, quarterly reviews, or boardroom discussions. But what if it could? What if real, authentic care for people was the missing piece to achieving the outcomes we've all been chasing?

Leadership is both a continuous learning experience and a tremendous responsibility. I have experienced this responsibility not only in my personal leadership at Amegy Bank, but also in the challenges I've observed among the business leaders we serve. There is an inherent contradiction when we try to balance discipline, accountability, results, and yes, even love. I've spent decades focusing on processes, metrics, and systems to drive performance, often keeping emotions at bay. It was safer, and honestly, it worked—until it didn't.

That's where *Love as a Business Strategy* comes in. Encouraged by a trusted friend, Donna Cole, I picked up this book, and I'll admit—I was hesitant. "Love" felt too soft, too personal. But by the second chapter, I was hooked. Mohammad Anwar and his team at Softway share their journey with a raw honesty that's rare. Their stories aren't just about profits or strategy; they are about leading with vulnerability, transforming their culture, and ultimately thriving through adversity.

Their reflections resonated with me, especially in my own work at Amegy Bank, where we face the challenge of building a culture that's both resilient and invested in each other. This book doesn't just present theories. It offers actionable steps for leaders to navigate the tension between driving results and fostering deep connection. It's an approach that aligns with what many of us are trying to achieve: a workplace where people show up as their full selves, invested not just in their work but in each other.

One of the book's greatest strengths is its ability to quantify the link between culture and business results. Mohammed and his leadership team's willingness to share their setbacks reminds us that we often learn more in failure than in success. This authenticity and passion to help others reflects an exemplary commitment to personal and professional growth.

Love as a Business Strategy stands out as one of my all-time favorite books. It's a must-read for leaders who strive to understand the interdependencies of strategy, culture, and behavior. The Culture+ team offers more than just advice—they offer a roadmap to creating a thriving business environment where results naturally follow. At Amegy, we're already seeing the shift as we apply these lessons to our own journey.

If you're ready to lead differently, I encourage you to read *Love as a Business Strategy* with an open mind. It's a call to transform how you lead, without abandoning discipline or strategy. Instead, it shows how combining these traits with empathy and connection can lead to truly sustainable success. The more I engage with the Culture+ team, the deeper my gratitude grows for their insights and support.

—Steve Stephens, CEO, Amegy Bank

Our Darkest Day

The last few people filed into the large conference room, and the director shut the door behind them with an ominous *click*.

The crowd of employees looked around, confused. No one knew why they were there. After a pause that felt like an eternity, an HR manager began handing out folders. One woman peeked into her folder and started reading. She looked as if she was going to cry.

A second director cleared his throat from the front of the room. "You're probably wondering why we called you here today," he said awkwardly. "Unfortunately, the company is going through a downturn. Effective immediately, everyone in this room is being let go."

Twenty voices erupted at once in shock and disbelief. The director gestured for silence, then continued. "In a few minutes, security will arrive outside the room, and you'll be taken out in small groups to pack your things. Then you'll be escorted out of the building."

A man in the front row scowled. Another asked, "Can I say good-bye to anyone?"

The director shook his head. "No. Anyone who is staying with the company is in a separate room. This is for everyone's protection."

"You can't just escort us out like criminals!" someone shouted.

The director's face was set. "The folder in your hands has all the details you'll need. We appreciate your work. Thank you."

Angry voices flooded the room once more. But as security arrived to escort the first group out, their protests gave way to resigned silence.

A woman came up to the director, hugging herself. "Why me?" she asked. "I'm good at what I do. I made it through the performance audit last month. Can you at least tell me why you picked me?"

The director looked at the woman and then toward security, but they were occupied. Reluctantly he turned back to her. "We needed to select a certain number of people. We did the best we could. There wasn't a reason you made the list. You just did."

"No *reason?* This is my livelihood! What do I tell my children?"

The director didn't feel good about brushing her off like that. *But this is how they told me to do it,* he told himself. *This is how you lay people off.*

He got security's attention, waved them over, and had them escort the woman out with the next group.

The director let out a small sigh of relief. He wouldn't get a wink of sleep that night, but at least the hard part was over.

It had been a sleepless few weeks for many of the higher-ups at Softway, especially for Mohammad, the company's founder, president, and CEO. Since 2003, Softway had been nothing but successful by all the standard metrics—revenue, profitability, year-on-year growth, you name it.

And yet, about a month prior to the layoffs, Softway's executive leadership team called a meeting with Mohammad to deliver some shocking news: Softway was in a bad place. The industry was in a downturn, the company was losing contracts, and they weren't bringing in enough new clients to make up the difference. For the company to survive, Mohammad would have to cut ties with over a third of the company's 260 employees.

Mohammad slumped in his chair, stunned. "Okay," he said. "Tell me what I need to do."

The executive leadership team walked him through the standard corporate layoff procedure: no one-on-one conversations, no apologies, no good-byes, and, above all, no actions or behaviors that might make Mohammad or Softway look sympathetic to their situation.

Mohammad swallowed hard, reminded himself of why he had hired this leadership team in the first place, and decided to take their advice.

Then he assembled his management team—including Frank and Jeff—to share the news and seek their help in deciding which employees to let go. This was going to be tough. To hit their quota, they would have to lay off some great performers.

Then came the day of the layoffs. The directors led one group to be laid off, while Mohammad, Frank, and Jeff led the remaining group to another room on the other side of the building—where no one could see what was happening to their coworkers.

Once all Softway's remaining employees were assembled, Mohammad addressed the group. "You've probably noticed that some of your friends are not in this room with you today. That is because they are no longer with the company."

Mohammad explained the tough situation Softway had found itself in. If the company hoped to remain in business, it would have to downsize. "But don't worry," Mohammad said, trying to sound upbeat. "If you're in this room, that means your job is safe."

"Yeah, for now," he heard a team member grumble from the back.

An hour or so later, the surviving team members emerged from the room and staggered back to their desks. All traces of their former colleagues were gone. Their desks were all cleaned out. Their tech accounts had been shut down. Even their lunches were missing from the fridge.

It was only eleven o'clock in the morning. On a Monday.

And Softway had just endured the darkest day in its history.

Business as Usual Sucks

If you picked up this book, our story probably sounds familiar. In fact, we're willing to bet that you or your organization have had at least one darkest day. Maybe you've had several. Or maybe one is on the way.

If so, know this: You're not alone.

Layoff stories like ours are far from unusual. In fact, all around the world, they're the norm. Just ask the executive leadership team who advised Mohammad. Every step was carefully planned to be as cold and dispassionate as possible. They knew exactly how to handle this process because they'd been down this road many times before.

But if the story of Softway's darkest day represents business as usual, then business as usual *sucks*.

Mohammad sensed this immediately as he oversaw the layoff process, and he began to question everything. What had his company become? Had he failed as a leader? Did Softway even deserve to continue?

These weren't easy questions to ask. After all, Mohammad loved being in business for himself. He'd grown the company from nothing to an eight-figure company with offices in America and India. But he knew he wasn't perfect. After all, he founded the company when he was only twenty, and he'd learned how to be a CEO on the fly. He knew he'd missed a lesson or two, which is why he'd recruited his executive leadership team to help him guide the company to the next level.

But that team was focused only on boosting the bottom line. The more aggressively they pursued this strategy, the more the company lost something far more valuable: its humanity.

Now, to be fair, culture had never been Softway's strong suit. But in the months leading up to our darkest day, the environment was so lifeless you could hear a pin drop. Softway employees saw their jobs as purely transactional. They would show up, get their work done, and then pack up and go home. We didn't know it yet, but we were living on borrowed time. Business as usual may have kept our doors open and our bank accounts healthy for a while, but eventually our balance came due.

Fortunately, since our darkest day Softway has learned not just to survive but to thrive—all thanks to an approach we call Love as a Business Strategy. Through it, we have rediscovered our humanity, put people at the center of work, and completely pivoted our business.

Love Is Good. . .for Business

In the chapters to come, we're going to share the story of how we discovered and adopted Love as a Business Strategy, what that pivot has created for us, and how you and your organization can do the same.

But first let's address the elephant in the room: What is *Love as a Business Strategy?* You'll get a complete description in Chapter 1, but in its simplest form, Love as a Business Strategy means creating a workplace that puts humanity first.

Here's why that matters: The average person spends more time with coworkers than with their own families. Work is the center of their lives. Far too often this sacrifice goes unacknowledged and unrewarded. Many organizations put little thought into the workplace environment they create, which often results in an indifferent or toxic culture. Eventually this culture seeps into other aspects of their employees' lives, affecting their health, family life, relationships, and happiness.

It doesn't have to be this way. People and profit don't have to be mutually exclusive. They can be complementary. After all, there is not one number on a balance sheet that isn't connected to a human being. If you want to produce better numbers over the long term, then it makes good business sense to support and empower the people *behind* those numbers.

Throughout this book, we explain how a culture of love leads to stronger, higher-performing teams; clearer, more attainable objectives; better business outcomes; and a healthier bottom line. This isn't just idle talk or well-intentioned theory. Both Softway and the organizations we consult with have seen firsthand how a people-first approach can drive quantifiable improvements across the board.

But while these results are both real and important for an organization's long-term success, they're only part of the story. In our experience, Love as a Business Strategy is worth pursuing if for no other reason than it's the right thing to do. If the only impact a culture of love has is that it improves workers' lives both inside *and* outside of work, it would still be worth it.

Lessons Grounded in Experience

This is not the first business book to discuss love, culture, or the importance of people. We acknowledge the input of so many others on our thinking, and we are indebted to their contributions. However, our journey has also helped us see things a little differently.

Since our darkest day in late 2015, Softway has become an entirely different company. We recognized that something needed to change, we committed to that change, and then we worked tirelessly to make that change a reality. Whatever we did before, we committed to doing the exact opposite—and that decision saved our company.

Along the way, a funny thing happened.

Inspired by our transformation, our clients began asking whether we could spark the same transformation within *their* organizations. Suddenly Love as a Business Strategy wasn't just something we practiced but something we taught as well. These early pilot programs eventually led to an inclusive leadership experience called Culture Rise, part of our offerings from Culture+, which we have shared with thousands of leaders and executives around the world.

Teaching Love as a Business Strategy was never part of the plan, but it has become a natural outgrowth of our work as our company. Our mission is to transform businesses the human way through technology, culture, and communications.

With this book, we share that mission with you.

This book is a collection of our lived experiences pursuing Love as a Business Strategy both at Softway and in our work with others. In the chapters to come, we offer practical approaches, sensible solutions, and immediate applications for creating a culture of love within your business. These understandings, mindsets, and behaviors are realistic and achievable, if not immediate. Each chapter is designed for you to understand and apply what you have learned in a real and tangible way.

To begin your journey, we start with the basics. In Part I, we take a deep dive into what we mean by Love as a Business Strategy—what it means, what it means for your culture, and why individual behaviors lie at the center of it all. Then in Part II, we introduce our Six Pillars of Love. Finally, in Part III, we put everything together and demonstrate how these concepts apply to different areas of your organization, such as leadership, teams and individuals, human resources, process and technology, business and people outcomes, and change management.

To bring these lessons to life, we share stories of our own journey of discovery, both before we embraced Love as a Business Strategy and after. Some of these stories detail our proudest moments, and some reveal our most unfortunate misbehaviors.

We share these stories not to brag—and certainly not to embarrass anyone—but to build empathy. We've experienced the cultural issues you're facing at your workplace, and we know what works and what doesn't. By telling our story human to human, employee to employee, leader to leader, our goal is to help you connect with our message so that you can apply it to your own situation and behavior. By understanding the emotional component of our journey and what is at stake, you will develop a clearer understanding of what is needed to make lasting behavior change within your own organization.

Do we have the data to make a business case for Love as a Business Strategy? Absolutely. But here's the thing: No one changes their behaviors because of data. They change when they understand the experience *behind* the data. When you lead with numbers, you neglect the people behind them. But when you lead with people, you allow the numbers to take care of themselves.

Finally, this is a book for both leaders and aspiring leaders—for anyone who manages people or who expects that they might one day. We've taught these lessons to organizations of all kinds—startups, midsize businesses, multinational corporations, private and public school systems, governments, and even nonprofits. Each has applied these lessons in its own different way. All have benefited.

But while Love as a Business Strategy has the power to transform organizations, the stories, lessons, and strategies laid out in this book can help at the individual level as well. We've especially found this to be true of middle managers, who occupy a unique position in their organizations. To those middle managers we say this: You may have the most to lose by standing up for change, but you also have the most to gain. After all, adding love to your work is a universal good, and the culture you create within your team can create a ripple effect throughout the rest of the organization.

Talking about love is easy. But delivering a culture of love in the workplace is hard work. Change doesn't happen overnight, and you *will* see a few setbacks along the way. We certainly did.

But although change doesn't happen overnight, it *is* possible—and it begins by embracing your own ability to affect that change. Whether you're the CEO of your company or the newest team member, you have influence. If you can learn to wield that influence in the service of a culture of love, you will find value both for yourself and for your organization. In fact, you may even find, as we did, that the impact you have is far greater than you could ever have imagined.

Welcome to the Second Edition

We first released *Love as a Business Strategy* in April 2021. Since then the journey this book has taken us on has been more rewarding than we ever could have imagined. It's led us to speaking opportunities at conferences, workshops, and other events all around the world. It's led us to surprise meetings with presidents of foreign countries. And it's led us to completely rethink our company, our products and services, and the value we bring to the world.

Most important of all, it's helped us to connect with people and to hear their stories at a scale we never could have imagined. There's nothing quite like receiving an email or seeing a post on LinkedIn and learning how the principles in this book impacted someone. One letter, from a man in Indonesia, described how this book led to him on a journey that would completely transform his life. That's powerful stuff, and it means the world to us.

This edition still contains all the same stories and lessons as the first edition (and Mohammad is still just as embarrassed about it as ever). But, like Frank, it's slimmed down a little since 2021. We've learned to get to the point just a little bit faster this time around.

We've also added a book club facilitation guide to the end of each chapter. When we published the first edition of the book, we hosted a book club at Softway to discuss it as a company. The conversations from those meetings helped set the stage for us to level up again, reassert our company's vision, and solidify our expectations for how we treat each other.

We believe it can do the same for you.

At the end of each chapter, you'll find an extensive list of questions crafted to maximize full-sentence answers rather than yes-or-no responses.

To be honest, we included a lot of questions. You're probably not going to walk through each and every question or conversation starter, but we wanted to give you options. Feel free to add, adjust, omit, refine, and/or use as is.

If you're a facilitator, here are a few things to keep in mind to keep the conversations running smoothly:

- Lead by example and share from a place of vulnerability. Setting the stage for others will also help them stay vulnerable, open to sharing, and leaning in.
- Take some time before your book club meeting to think through your own personal stories that you can connect to the stories and themes in the book.
- Consider the voices in the room (in person or virtually) who aren't being heard or may not feel comfortable speaking up. As facilitator, do your best to create equity in speaking time among book club members. If a few voices dominate the

conversation, make sure to prompt folks who haven't gotten a chance to share.

We hope the conversations that stem from your discussions are refreshing and empowering.

Questions for "Our Darkest Day"

- ◆ Have you experienced a "dark day" like the one described? If so, what happened? How did it impact morale?
- ◆ If you could wave a magic wand, how would you have run those layoffs?
- ◆ Why do you think Mohammad listened to the advice of his executive team?
- ◆ Why do you believe business can be so heartless?
- ◆ Based on what you know now (having read this section), how can love be good for business?
- ◆ What were some of your takeaways from this introductory chapter to the book?
- ◆ After reading this chapter, are you skeptical about how we define "Love as a Business Strategy"? If so, share those thoughts with the group.
- ◆ What were some of your biggest *ah-ha* moments from this chapter?
- ◆ Share a moment of self-awareness about your leadership after reading this chapter.
- ◆ What, if anything, will you change or adjust about how you lead or behave based on what you've read?

PART I

Why Love Is Good for Business

Do you enjoy working with jerks? Neither do we.

Even jerks that are really good at their jobs make work unbearable. Sure, some may get work done, but they don't lift anyone else up in the process. Are they aware of how their behaviors affect others? Probably not. But that begs the question: Are *you* aware of how *your* behaviors affect the people around you?

The work of building resilient, high-performing companies starts at the individual level. This is why behaviors are the core of Softway's business philosophy. How we treat each other creates or destroys culture. To build what we call a *culture of love*, every member of an organization must work toward improving their behaviors—both to better themselves and to make work more bearable for others.

Through introspection and self-awareness, meaningful behavior change is possible. Amplified by the Six Pillars of Love (which we cover in Part II), we're able to achieve resilience and belonging, which in turn leads to our goal of high-performing teams and better business outcomes (lookin' at you, Part III).

So here it is. Our secret sauce, on full display in one handy figure before you even turn to Chapter 1. This is the philosophy we actively practice to cultivate a culture of love within the walls of Softway and what we share with our clients too. We have stress-tested this framework with organizations of all kinds, all over the world, and we have structured this book to mirror it. In Part I, we start by tackling the foundational component of this philosophy: behaviors. But before we get there, we have to talk about the elephant in the room: What does love even mean?

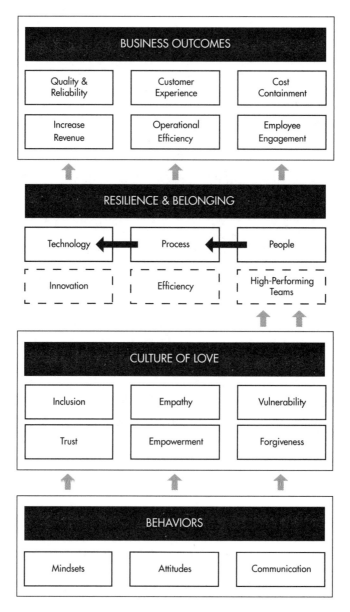

Figure P1.1 LAAS Framework

CHAPTER 1

What Is Love? (Baby Don't Hurt Me)

In November 2015, Softway had its darkest day. Confronted with an unexpected downturn and desperate to keep his company afloat, Mohammad agreed to lay off over a third of Softway's workforce—around a hundred employees in all. This grim reality, coupled with the dehumanizing layoff process and the very real prospect that he might still lose his company, led Mohammad to a prolonged period of soul-searching.

It was in this introspective mood that Mohammad found himself at a University of Houston football game (that's American football, for all you international readers) a few weeks after Softway's layoffs. Mohammad's alma mater, the University of Houston, had put together a surprisingly successful season under rookie head coach Tom Herman. In fact, the undefeated Cougars had even cracked the top 25 in rankings, according to an AP poll. On this particular Saturday afternoon, the University of Houston was set to square off against the University of Memphis Tigers. It was a big game, the biggest the Cougars had played in a long time.

Maybe this game would be the distraction Mohammad needed to take his mind off his failing company.

Or maybe not.

The first few quarters did not go well for the Cougars. After losing their starting quarterback early in the game, and with their second-string quarterback already on the injured list, the team trotted out their third-string quarterback. This third-stringer couldn't keep his head in the game; he seemed just as surprised to be playing as the fans were seeing him play.

As the fourth quarter began, U of H was down 14–34, with about a 0.1 percent chance of winning, according to ESPN. Mohammad watched as the fans around him stood up and headed home. He couldn't blame them, but something told him to stick around a few more minutes and see if the Cougars had one more miracle left.

Over the next eleven-plus minutes, the Cougars began playing like a team possessed—making play after play, pass after pass, run after run, until they pulled ahead by a point and held on to win the game.

Greatest. Comeback. Ever.

When you witness a game like that, the experience has a way of bleeding over into everything else that's going on in your life. Mohammad couldn't help but draw a parallel between the challenge U of H had just overcome and the challenge he faced at Softway. Here in November 2015, the company was both literally and figuratively in its fourth quarter. It was down by a lot, and the odds weren't good, but the game wasn't over.

For the first time in months, Mohammad felt a glimmer of hope that maybe, just maybe, Softway could pull off a miraculous win of its own. That night, he vowed to fight for the future of his company with everything he had.

On Monday, still feeling the high of Saturday's game, Mohammad logged onto Facebook to watch Coach Herman address the press.

"You talk about how much these guys love each other," one reporter said. "We don't hear that a lot in the football world. Is that something you wanted to instill here? And is that something that helps win games—like this Saturday—and win championships?"

Herman agreed, saying that love was crucial to the Cougars' success. He had played on, played against, and watched teams that looked great on paper but were only average on the field. "To say that you are going to be elite or championship level in this sport without a genuine love and care for the guy next to you, I don't think it can happen," he said.

The reporter asked a follow-up: What exactly did he mean by "love" in the context of football?

"It's not 'Yo Love you, Dawg!' love," Herman explained. "It's a kiss you on your cheek, squeeze you real tight, and tell you, 'You have my heart in your hands' love....We're into real genuine love—and that's the only way I know how to do it. And it's the only way *we* know how to do it. And it's paid off so far."

Coach Herman's comments stopped Mohammad dead in his tracks. He had never heard a coach—or anyone—talk about "love" that way. But maybe Coach Herman was on to something. After all, the rookie coach had just guided a team with few star-quality players to a 10–0 start to the season. They had overperformed at every turn, often in dramatic fashion.

Mohammad turned off the press conference and sat silently at his desk. Was he like Coach Herman? Did he love *his* team? Admittedly, he did not. Mohammad could describe Softway's culture and his relationship to it in a lot of ways, but none of those ways included words like "love," "support," or "compassion."

But why not? Why couldn't Softway create a culture of love like the Cougars had? If love was the advantage they needed to become a winning team, why couldn't it be the business advantage that would drive Softway's own comeback story?

The more Mohammad thought about it, the more he saw love as a viable path forward. He wanted a team that didn't need to rely on star players to be excellent, a team that could overcome odds and take on any challenge, a team that radiated resilience, embraced challenges, and didn't believe in no-win scenarios. And he was willing to do whatever it took to make it happen.

Time to Fight

On that Monday, Mohammad heard Coach Herman use the words "culture of love" for the first time. On Friday, he was using that phrase himself in an all-hands company-wide meeting.

Everyone gathered for the call, with the American team members all packed into the company's large conference room and the Indian team members joining in over video. No one knew for sure what the meeting was about, but most assumed Mohammad would be announcing Softway's permanent closure.

As everyone got settled, Mohammad took a deep breath and then uttered the one sentence no one could have possibly expected: "I love you all."

The room let out a gasp. Surely this was not the real Mohammad. Had he swapped bodies with a lookalike? Was this a *Freaky Friday* kind of situation?

Mohammad let the surprise pass, then he continued. First, he told them about the University of Houston football game. Then he told them about Coach Herman's emphasis on love in creating winning teams. Finally he explained that, from that day forward, Softway would be going all in on creating its own culture of love.

"We need to love and support each other," Mohammad said. "That's the only way we will get through this."

No one was sure what to make of Mohammad's speech, but they could tell he was serious and committed to taking the company in this new direction. While the path forward was uncertain, the change in the room was unmistakable. Suddenly it was okay to be optimistic again. It was okay to care. It was okay to feel inspired. It was okay to *try*, to fight not only for the company's survival but for their teammates' futures.

And with love as their guide, it was okay to believe that they just might win.

Love Is. . .

Since that November day in 2015, love has been at the center of everything Softway does, impacting not only our culture but also our products and services, our relationships with clients, and even our position in the business world.

But, just as the artist Haddaway wondered in his popular '90s dance hit, we have to know: What is love? What exactly do we mean when we say we want to bring humanity back to the workplace?

First, let's get the obvious out of the way: Love in the workplace isn't about romantic love. It isn't about hugs and kisses either. An invitation to create a culture of love is *not* an invitation to drop a dumpster fire on your HR department.

Love as a Business Strategy means embracing a deep-rooted and intrinsic care for other humans. It means working as a team and prioritizing honest, kind, and transparent communication. It means putting other people before yourself. It means looking to the person on your right and on your left and asking what is best for them, not just what's best for you. It means working toward and celebrating our shared humanity, not just chasing profits.

. . .A RIPPLE EFFECT

Before Mohammad's fateful experience at the University of Houston game, love didn't drive our business. Greed did.

To be blunt, the massive round of layoffs we experienced in 2015 was the logical outcome of a poorly run company and an indifferent executive leadership team. Driving this executive leadership team was Mohammad, whose own marginalizing and diminishing behavior may have been the worst of all. Most days Mohammad would acknowledge you only if he needed something from you or if he wanted to yell at you (even if the problem wasn't your fault). And those were the good days.

These behaviors had an impact on organizational culture. Camaraderie between employees was practically nonexistent. Smiles and banter were reserved for lunch breaks far from the office. No one had a sense of shared purpose in what they were doing. Before the layoffs, no one even knew the company was in trouble.

Mohammad now understood that he had shaped this dismal culture through his own actions. As the president and CEO, his behaviors had an outsize impact on the experiences and behaviors of others, and he had not taken responsibility for his behaviors seriously.

Organizations succeed when humans can come together to work, collaborate, and achieve beyond any single person's vision or ability. None of this can happen in a restrained environment. We understand this intuitively, and yet we often don't stop to consider the kind of environment we want to create for ourselves and others. Sure, we may realize that the workplace can be a little lifeless, but we ignore how dangerous that is. Silence is not a sign of work getting done. It's a sign of impending doom.

Fortunately, if a culture of greed is defined by individual behaviors, so is a culture of love:

- Love means doing things out of care for others and with the intent of helping others, even if those things aren't easy.
- Love means not sweeping problems under the rug.

- ◆ Love means working toward inclusion rather than reinforcing hierarchy.
- ◆ Love means embracing the hard conversations rather than avoiding them.
- ◆ Love means building processes, tools, and policies that align people with profit.
- ◆ Love means support, accountability, and trust, which leads to innovation, efficiency, and measurable business outcomes.

This isn't to say that a culture of love is all sunshine and roses. In fact, as you'll see throughout this book, creating this culture is hard work. But the difference in your business between a culture of greed and a culture of love is the difference between a team of all-stars and an all-star team. Just as Coach Herman proved at the University of Houston, teams of individualistic all-stars rarely outperform teams of players who work together as a unit. Why? Because while all-stars often act in their own self-interest, all-star *teams* act out of love and a sense of mutual support.

What Is Your Workplace Environment Like?

Pursuing Love as a Business Strategy requires self-awareness and reflection about your own environment and behaviors. Here are a few basic questions to get you started:

- ◆ What does the environment in your own workplace look like?
- ◆ Is your workplace—whether physical or virtual—lively or silent?
- ◆ Do team members walk on eggshells around each other, especially around managers and leaders?
- ◆ Do team members spend long hours overpolishing presentations that decision makers will barely pay attention to?

If your current work environment is heavy on politics but light on genuine interaction, then it's likely you don't work in a culture of love.

. . .SPEAKING TRUTH TO POWER

"You made me feel like I wasn't worth your time," Maggie said quietly.

Chris, Maggie's supervisor, sighed. "I'm sorry I made you feel like that. You're right. You'd rescheduled the meeting twice for me, and. . ."

". . .then you didn't show up at all. Without even sending me an email," Maggie said.

Chris stared at the floor. It was 2019. Softway's culture of love wasn't a baby anymore. Chris knew better than to treat Maggie like this. He also knew he needed to make the situation right. Unfortunately, he also had a plane to catch. As much as it pained him to do so, he had to leave Maggie waiting once again.

Maggie sighed. She had been terrified to confront Chris. However, now a year into her role as a project manager, she had fully bought in to Softway's culture of love. If she wanted to uphold that culture, she needed to hold Chris accountable so that he would understand how badly his actions were setting her back in her own work.

That night Maggie told her roommate how she had called Chris out for standing her up for another meeting.

Her roommate stared at her. "Wait, what?"

"What?" Maggie said innocently.

"Chris, a vice president, who could fire you on the spot—that Chris? You really talked to him like that?"

"Um, sure," Maggie said, a little uncomfortable. "What's wrong with that?"

Everything, according to Maggie's roommate. "Sometimes honesty isn't the best policy if you want to keep your job."

Maggie was touched that her roommate was trying to take care of her—and in a normal organization, her roommate would have been right. Softway, however, wasn't a normal organization. . .at least, so she hoped. *Had* she done the right thing? Suddenly she had second thoughts.

The next day a huge bouquet of colorful flowers arrived at her desk. The card was from Chris: "I'm sorry. You are absolutely worth my time."

Maggie smiled, brought the flowers home, and put the bouquet in her kitchen.

Chris continued to follow up on his apology with action, making the next ten one-on-ones with Maggie on time and without incident. (He had to reschedule the eleventh, but he emailed Maggie *days* in advance to move it.)

Maggie had done the right thing after all.

When we share this story with leaders at other organizations, they are often just as shocked as Maggie's roommate. They worry that allowing their employees to speak truth to power endangers their authority. This idea couldn't be further from the truth. If the Maggies of our organization lose their sense of safety and permission, then we as a company lose the ability to talk about real issues.

Speaking truth to power isn't about challenging authority for the sake of it, and it's certainly not about giving leaders a piece of your mind. Love doesn't speak out of disrespect. Instead, love is about being receptive and empathetic. It's about approaching people as fellow humans, regardless of title or who is sitting in what chair. When everyone is on the same side, then everyone's contribution matters; and when everyone's contribution matters, then everyone will take care to communicate compassionately and effectively.

Speaking truth to power is both emotionally healthy and more efficient. Consider your own experience for a moment. Has there ever been a time where you wanted to raise a flag within your company, but you weren't sure how to deliver the message? How much time and anguish went into planning out what you wanted to say? However much time that was, it was too much—especially if you never got up the nerve to say anything.

Now, if you're a leader, here's another question: Have you ever thought about what someone's silence is costing you?

Spoiler alert: The answer is *a lot.*

Consider this true story of the top-level executive who, after sitting through a presentation on a new branding design, said, "Huh. I thought that would be blue instead of red."

The executive was just thinking out loud, more curious than anything else. But because that organization's culture was rooted in fear and silence, that one comment was akin to a four-alarm fire. Suddenly entire teams within the company mobilized to change all the reds to blues—without ever asking the executive if that's what he wanted. He didn't; he was indifferent. But because no one felt empowered to open that dialogue with him, a lot of time, money, and resources were wasted.

In fear-based organizations, many conversations around strategy and behavior become events. You have to plan for them, use the right words, and include the right imagery. You have to make sure you're brand compliant. You have to be so, so careful to say everything correctly and at the right time.

That's a lot of work, effort, and mental energy spent on essentially spinning your wheels. Why can't we just have a conversation without beating around the bush? Why can't we just be candid and not be offended?

Organizations that don't keep open communication channels, that don't encourage their employees to speak truth to power, are less effective and less efficient. Give your team members the space to feel safe enough to speak. Flush the issues out in the open so you can understand them, unite around them, take ownership of them, and then work together to solve them.

In a culture where you're encouraged to speak truth to power, success belongs to everyone, not just to leadership. The result is an engaged workforce that is invested in your organization's future. Everyone cares about cost containment. Everyone cares about sales. Everyone is committed to seeing the important numbers move, watching for trouble, and looking for opportunity. And when someone sees that something isn't right, or that something is objectively hurting those goals and values, they know that they are encouraged and empowered to speak up.

. . .SHARING AND LEARNING FROM MISTAKES

At a campus Jeff once worked on many years ago, the company proudly displayed one of those "X days without an accident" signs. Jeff went past the sign twice a day, and twice a day he had a positive reaction when he saw any number larger than zero. It felt good to celebrate safe days on campus.

Years later Jeff realized how counterproductive those signs were. They didn't promote safety. They promoted fear.

The core of this issue is what Harvard scholar Amy Edmondson has called *psychological safety*. Edmondson first coined the term during her work in the medical field, observing the ways in which doctors and nurses worked together in teams. As she discovered, the doctors and nurses who felt more comfortable with each other still made mistakes just like any professionals. However, because they were more willing to share and learn from each others' mistakes, other team members were less likely to make the same mistakes.[1]

Let's apply this lesson to Jeff's "X days without an accident" sign. Imagine you worked for this company. If you're the person who had an accident, how would you feel about resetting the counter? You'd probably be pretty embarrassed—perhaps enough to avoid reporting the incident.

This is what a culture of fear looks like. Accident counters may have good intentions, but they create the opposite results from what they're intended for. In a culture of fear, the accident *is* the failure. When people are afraid to even disclose that they had an accident, they fail to share any meaningful lessons they learned with the rest of their team, thereby dooming other teammates to make similar mistakes.

A culture of love doesn't use counters and fear to encourage employee safety. Instead, it uses transparency and open communication. It encourages team members to talk about every safety incident openly—even the close calls—so that the focus is on learning rather than blaming.

Love Ain't Easy

When Mohammad called that all-hands meeting and, to the shock of the company's remaining workforce, took a stand for love, Softway's problems didn't magically disappear, and our culture didn't change overnight. The transformation took time—and we're still working on it.

The important work always takes time. There are a lot of variables to account for. As a leader, Mohammad had to learn what it meant to embody a culture of love, to establish it as the core strategy of his business, and to develop the mindsets and practices that would allow him to sustain the effort.

Doing that takes time—just as it took time for Mohammad to generate the kind of buy-in that would lead to organizational transformation. When he delivered his speech in favor of a culture of love, nearly everyone in the company agreed that his message helped clear the air and inspire the company to dig in and fight for its survival. However, there's a big difference between an inspirational speech and the hard, messy work of making the tenets of that speech the defining traits of your identity and culture.

Everyone loves a catalyzing moment. Everyone loves excitement and feeling inspired. However, once the big moment subsides, you're left with either empty words or hard actions.

Some folks at the company were certain it would be the former, that Mohammad was just riding a high from a great football game and that his enthusiasm would peter out in a month or so. They'd seen leadership wave at other flavor-of-the-month initiatives before, and they had little reason to think this time would be any different.

But when Mohammad started walking the talk, there was no longer any room for debate: He meant business—and business meant love.

That's when the blowback began and team members began second-guessing Mohammad's actions and intentions. Many left—including the executives who had overseen the layoffs that led to our darkest day. They were unconvinced of the value of Love as a Business strategy and refused to embrace it.

The concept of Love as a Business Strategy is not built with words. It's built out of consistent daily action. It requires a focus on strong, inclusive relationships that are rooted in truth and mutual respect. It's a long process, and often it's a messy one. But it works.

As we stared down our own fourth quarter in 2015, worried about going bankrupt, at times it felt like our odds for success were about 0.1 percent. At one point, we didn't even have enough cash in the bank to make payroll that week. But slowly we clawed our way back. A year later we were a profitable business again, and love had begun to take root in every aspect of our operation, from our strategic approach, to our culture and behavior, and to the very way we organized as a company.

A year after the layoffs, Mohammad wrote an open letter to his company. In it he recounted the experience that had kicked off the company's journey of love and reflected on how far the company had come. Once again he told the story of his experience at the University of Houston game, how he had left the game feeling fired up and ready to save his company, and how Coach Herman's emphasis on love had served as his inspiration for Softway's journey. The company had long since embraced his vision, but the letter served as a crystallizing moment, punctuated by these final lines:

I hope you guys have enjoyed reading my story about how the Houston Cougars have inspired me! I look forward to reading your stories about who [inspired you. . .] and how you have adapted what inspires you to your lives.

Take care and I love you all very much!!!

Just a year prior, Mohammad had looked deep into his soul and stared down an ugly truth: He didn't love his company and the people he worked with. Now he was engaging his team members as if they were his best friends, sharing his greatest passions, encouraging others to do the same, and emphasizing his love and support for them.

For the rest of the Softway team reading this message, Mohammad's passion and sincerity were unmistakable. It was hard to believe that this was the same person who had once written the company a very different sort of letter—a letter that will forever live in Softway infamy.

Questions for "What Is Love? (Baby Don't Hurt Me)"

- ◆ When you first heard/read the book title, what was your first reaction?
- ◆ Think back to the framework in the beginning of Part I, and share your thoughts about the framework. Do you believe that "behaviors are the bottom line"? Why or why not?
- ◆ What does the environment of your workplace look like? What does it *feel* like?
- ◆ Is your organization operating from a culture of greed or a culture of love? Share some examples for either culture.
- ◆ What's it like to experience a culture of fear? How does a culture like that impact you, your peers, and your workplace?
- ◆ When you speak truth to power, what happens? If you're in a leadership position, how do you respond when someone speaks the truth to you?
- ◆ Out of all the examples of what love really looks like at work, which one resonates the most with you?

Love means. . .

- Doing things out of care for others.
- Not sweeping problems under the rug.
- Working toward inclusion.
- Embracing hard conversations.
- Aligning people with profit.
- Support, accountability, and trust.

◆ After reading this chapter, do you hesitate to introduce a culture of love to your team/department/organization? Explain your answer.

◆ What were some of your biggest takeaways or *ah-ha* moments from this chapter?

◆ Share a moment of self-awareness about your own leadership after reading this chapter.

◆ What, if anything, will you change or adjust about how you lead based on what you've read?

Note

1. See Charles Duhigg, "What Google Learned from Its Quest to Build the Perfect Team," *New York Times Magazine*, February 25, 2016. www.nytimes.com/2016/02/28/magazine/what-google-learned-from-its-quest-to-build-the-perfect-team.html

CHAPTER 2

Culture Eats Strategy for Breakfast

It's lunchtime in the Softway office. You head over to the break room and open the fridge. After pushing a few things around, you find your food, grab a spot at a nearby table, and start to eat.

A few minutes later, the CEO walks in. Clearly distracted by something, he opens the fridge, mumbles something under his breath, slams the door shut, and storms out. *That's odd*, you think. *Must not have been hungry, I guess.*

You finish lunch, head back to your desk, and log back on. Immediately, you notice a message in your inbox from your CEO—and it's a doozy:

Hello Team, It's really disgusting to see our fridge. There were items like Empty Bags, Last loaf of bread with mold, Empty Milk Cartons, Sauces, rotten bananas and these Boxes with food for DAYS AND DAYS all together. . . Really ?? Is this the hygiene you guys follow in your own homes? Disgusting! Here is the deal—We as a company are not required to provide you with a refrigerator. If you guys cannot take your own trash out the fridge on a regular basis.. I will not continue to tolerate this. You may do what ever you please with your own refrigerators. But you are not allowed to Softway's Refrigirators as your science experiment lab!!! I will give time till this noon for the folks who would like to reclaim their lunch boxes to take them or they will be thrown in the Trash!! This just demonstrates the lack of hygiene, discipline, and it shows How LAZY some of you guys can be to throw trash. I mean EMPTY BAGS and EMPTY MILK CARTONS??? SERIOUSLY??? I also would like an acknowledgement reply to this email that you all understand that we need to keep our refrigerators clean by end of day today. The ones who do not respond to my email will have to help me clean the fridge tomorrow! Thank You!

Oof. That's not a good look. But hey, at least Mohammad said "thank you" at the end.

No doubt, you've received an email very similar to the very real message—typos included—Mohammad sent out that day. The details may be different, but the result is the same: a toxic, dehumanizing company culture.

Mohammad got what he wanted out of this email. In the hours after he sent it, team members descended on the break room in a mad dash to clean up their mess and make the refrigerator look spotless for their CEO. But Mohammad's victory was short-lived: The refrigerator was filthy again a few weeks later.

Mohammad's hollow victory came at a tremendous cost. Team members weren't merely afraid to bring food to work now. Many had completely lost faith in their CEO. We know this because they told us so (and the rest of the world) on Glassdoor. Just look at this glowing review:

The upper management is completely unprofessional. Expect to be ridiculed, yelled at, or cursed. You can also look forward to petty emails about the condition of the refrigerator with demands that you meet to clean it (which you may not even use). . .If you see any good reviews, you can assume they're written by HR!

There are plenty more reviews like this on Glassdoor and other sites. They're embarrassing to read and hurt our ability to hire new talent. But we earned those reviews, and we hold ourselves accountable to them. This is who we were before our pivot—a toxic, psychologically unsafe culture that drove away good people in droves.

This was a culture of our own making. While culture may be perpetuated by every team member in an organization, it begins with leadership. We had failed to produce and perpetuate a culture that we were proud of.

Without an intense, committed, and consistent focus on culture, Love as a Business Strategy does not work. But to create a culture of love, first it's important to understand what exactly culture is and why it matters so much to an organization's success.

Culture Is. . .

Defining "culture" can be tricky. Broadly, we define culture as the emotional environment you create and the behaviors that build it—whether those behaviors are toxic or supportive. Culture can be the passive-aggressive nastygram your CEO sends out about refrigerator etiquette. Or culture can be the praise someone shares about you during a big meeting. In either case, culture is like the Force in *Star Wars*. We can't see it, but we can feel its presence in everything.

If you or your team members consistently dread going to work, then you have a bad culture. Team members play politics all day. They rush to get work done and go home. There's no camaraderie, no mutual support, no interest in anything other than performing their job at a bare-bones level and collecting their next paycheck. They are complacent and unsatisfied.

If you or your team members *like* going to work, then you probably have a good culture. People treat each other as human beings and are confident that others will treat them the same. They are empowered to make proactive decisions. They are entrusted to do the right thing. They are included and welcome to disagree. They are free to bring their full selves to work.

That's it in a nutshell. But there's more to it than that. Let's dive into some specifics.

. . .NOT PERKS AND BENEFITS

Can you describe your company culture without mentioning your perks and benefits?

Companies love to showcase all their shiny bells and whistles in their recruiting materials. But as wonderful as an on-campus ice cream shop or a state-of-the-art gym is, they're just perks—and perks aren't the same as culture. A break room ping-pong table alone doesn't create a workforce of engaged contributors. Instead, perks and benefits like this often create a hostage situation.

We know one person, we'll call her Anna, who stayed at a job that she hated for over five years. Why? Because she loved her perks and benefits and worried that she wouldn't get them anywhere else. The irony, of course, is that she was too busy to ever enjoy those perks. And if somebody else dared to enjoy the ping-pong table while she was chasing a deadline, it made her blood boil.

This illusion of culture and support kept Anna at her desk for a while, but eventually she wised up and left.

Anna's experience is not unique. Companies that mistake perks and benefits for culture generally have a miserable workforce with a high turnover rate. As a result, HR must lie through their teeth every day just to recruit people into the company. We know because that's what our HR team did. And we couldn't blame them. When everyone's miserable and already has one foot out the door, eventually you run out of honest reasons to convince people to come in.

> Leaders focusing on perks and benefits alone don't create a workforce of engaged contributors. Instead, they create a hostage situation.

. . .GROWTH AND EMPOWERMENT

Famed business leader Peter Drucker once said that culture eats strategy for breakfast. What Drucker meant by this is that a well-conceived plan is meaningless if your team isn't united around that plan. Drucker understood that culture has an uncanny ability to motivate and unite people.

We agree that culture eats strategy for breakfast. But, as we discuss in more detail in the next chapter, we also say that *behavior eats culture for lunch*. Why? Because culture is the result of individual behaviors built up over time. In a culture of love, team members make proactive decisions about how to conduct themselves.

The question is, how do you measure culture? How do you know you're doing a good job promoting and growing a culture of love?

It's not easy. After all, measuring culture is more than just determining how many high-fives Jeff handed out in a day. While engagement measurement tools can give you a good sense of satisfaction and motivation, typically they stop short of measuring actual experiences. Tools like this are a nice start, but they don't help you understand *why* or *where* your culture is either struggling or thriving.

We couldn't find a tool that truly measured culture in a meaningful way and aligned with our Love as a Business Strategy Framework, so we built one for anyone to use. (See Part I, "Why Love Is Good for Business.") Broadly speaking, the Culture Counter tool (www.Culture Counter.app) allows us to measure to key benchmarks of culture: growth and empowerment. In a healthy culture, team members are:

◆ Encouraged to communicate, be open, and share their perspective and ideas.
◆ Secure in the belief that no matter what their identity or background, their contributions are valued and their voice matters.
◆ Able to be forgiven for mistakes and misbehavior.
◆ Able to give and receive feedback freely.

Is a healthy culture a workplace utopia? Of course not. Nobody wakes up excited to go to work every single day. No workplace is composed entirely of flawless communicators. Practicing love and applying it to culture is messy. That's just part of being human.

However, the difference is that, in a healthy culture, when you wake up feeling dread about a particular aspect of your job that day, that feeling doesn't represent the entire experience of your work life. If you have a messy interaction with a teammate, you know you have the tools, resources, and space to address that interaction and grow from it. Finally, and perhaps most important, you believe that your work is engaging, your skills are put to good use, and the work you do matters. . .even if you don't *love* every single task you perform.

If you're not sure whether your organization has a healthy culture, here's a shortcut. Ask yourself: If your organization was on the verge of closing its doors, would you dig in and fight, or would you jump ship? People fight for what they believe in. Nobody but the owner fights for an organization with a bad culture.

Gaining a Full View of Your Culture

There's more than one reason to care about your company culture. With the rise of workplace review sites like Glassdoor and Kanarys, your culture is on display for the world to see—a fact that can meaningfully impact your ability to recruit talent.

Glassdoor has become the standard that companies are held against, but other sites measure company culture in other useful ways. Kanarys, for instance, rates companies on diversity and inclusion. For those in historically minority or under-served communities, this can be an invaluable tool in deciding where to work.

If you have big goals for HR, particularly around diversity in recruiting, be careful that your approach to diversity, equity, inclusion, and belonging isn't just empty words. If you want to be known as a good place to work, then walk the talk.

Anyone Can Influence Culture

Culture is embodied in every interaction with every person. Day by day, action by action, we build each other up or tear each other down, and make space for others to do the same. Never is this more important than when we're talking about leaders.

Leaders have an outsize influence. Leaders set the tone. This is true in families, in business, and in politics. Every time a leader models the values and behaviors of a culture of love, their organization takes another step in a healthy direction. Conversely, every time a leader misbehaves, the culture is damaged. There are no neutral interactions.

When Mohammad sent out his infamous refrigerator email, he sent the organization a crystal-clear picture of what kinds of behaviors were acceptable at Softway in 2015. Leaving a mess in the fridge was unacceptable, but publicly berating other team members was fair game. Had Mohammad thought through the consequences of his behaviors, he probably would have found another way to ask his team to clean the refrigerator—perhaps by leading by example and cleaning it himself.

That said, leadership doesn't always happen at the top. Anyone can influence culture. If you're in middle management or an individual contributor on your team, you can still make a difference in the values and behaviors that you choose to model.

Consider the example of Priyanka, a recruiter at Softway's Bengaluru office. For years, Priyanka had no interest in veering outside of her core competency. If the task didn't say "recruiting," in its description, she wouldn't touch it.

As Priyanka and other team members in HR shared their struggles and successes with each other, they realized that their insights didn't only impact the world of recruiting, but also payroll, communication, and leadership. This experience opened their eyes, and as a department, HR began weighing in on conversations and contributing to work that extended well beyond recruiting.

When other departments saw this shift, they wanted to bring this change to their own team. Soon Priyanka and her team were offering support and coaching to other teams who wanted to take a more cross-functional approach to their work. Ultimately, this one culture change—driven by leadership, internalized by individual contributors, and evangelized within their teams—ended up dramatically impacting Softway's culture.

No one works with a thousand people every day. Most people interact with about three to five other team members daily and perhaps ten to fifteen people over the course of a week. But you can have an outsize influence on the ten to fifteen people you work most closely with—and those ten to fifteen people can do the same. Add up these efforts over time, and that's a lot of change.

It doesn't matter if you have a company of a hundred or 200,000. Change depends on individual actions. One person can change a team. One team can change a department. One department can change an organization. Progress isn't always linear, but it can be made.

Anyone Can Adapt to Culture

Frank gripped the passenger-side door in terror, barely suppressing a scream.

His life flashed before his eyes. Actually, no, it was a car, then a bicycle, then a rickshaw, then. . .a chicken? Screams, horns, and even the sounds of livestock filled the air.

Everywhere he looked, Frank saw only chaos. At the center of this chaos was Taj, Mohammad's brother and the managing director of Softway's Bengaluru office in India, who was laughing like a madman. Frank watched helplessly as Taj gunned the engine, hopped the car onto the sidewalk—on the *wrong side of the road*—and deftly wove between the many obstacles in his path.

Frank considered it a small miracle when the pair arrived at the hotel. After taking a moment to collect his wits, Frank looked over at Taj and said, "What the heck was that? I thought I was going to die!"

Taj laughed. "That's how you drive in India."

He was right. In the context of his culture and surroundings, Taj's crazy driving (of which he is *very* proud) was entirely normal. In fact, it was essential. Had he driven more conservatively, he might have *truly* put Frank in danger.

Frank understands that now. But still, he'll never ride with Taj again.

Taj takes no offense. He understands how his driving must seem to outsiders. People from different cultures behave in different ways.

So, when he first learned of Softway's pivot to a culture of love, Taj resisted. "That might work in America," he told Mohammad, "but there is no way it will work in India. That's not how Indians work."

Determined to change his brother's mind, Mohammad invited Taj to the United States for a visit. Upon his arrival, Mohammad let Taj take the wheel and drive back to the Houston office. It was as if a completely different man sat behind the wheel. *This* Taj obeyed the traffic laws, stuck to the speed limit, and stayed off the sidewalk.

"Do you see how you're driving right now?" Mohammad asked. Taj nodded. "You were raised to drive very differently in India. And yet you drive completely differently in Houston. Why do you think that is?"

Taj could see the point his brother was trying to make. If he could adapt to American traffic laws, then Softway's India division could similarly adapt to a culture of love.

Like Taj, leaders around the globe often incorrectly assume that what works in their primary office won't work in their satellite offices in Europe, Japan, India, or elsewhere. So, they try to "adapt" to different regional cultures by superficially decorating their offices in an "authentic" manner. Then, when those locations inevitably run into cultural conflicts or contradictions, American leadership blames the problem on the actions or behaviors of people "typical" of that region.

Not only is this wrong, but it's also insensitive. No matter what larger culture their team members might belong to, no matter how many offices they have in different locations around the world, organizations can still build a company culture that is consistent both among team members and across locations.

Still don't believe us? Consider your own behaviors for a moment. If you have a client-facing role, what do you do before visiting their office? If you're like us, you learn about their culture, norms, and safety standards ahead of time. If they require formal dress, you wear formal dress (even if the meeting is virtual). If they require that you leave your cell phone at the door, then you leave your cell phone at the door. From the moment you step onto their campus to the moment you're back in your car, you automatically change your behavior in the way their culture demands.

Like Taj when he's in Houston, like us when we're client-facing, if you can adjust your behaviors in different cultural contexts, then the rest of your team can too. No matter where your offices are located, no matter who the people are who work, every single member of your team is capable of behaving according to the values and behaviors mandated by a culture of love.

But for that to happen, those values and behaviors must be clearly articulated and enforced. So what exactly are the values and behaviors mandated by a culture of love? We'll get to that in Part II. But before we do, we need to understand the mindsets, behaviors, and attitudes that often stand in our way.

There's an App for That!

Since the dawn of the universe, since the formation of the Milky Way, since humans first learned to grunt at each other, one question has plagued us: How do you measure workplace culture?

We've cracked the code.

Softway's Culture Counter app can diagnose your organizational culture through the measurement of ten key behaviors. Through the app's intuitive dashboards, you'll get unparalleled insights into both your overarching culture and specific team dynamics. Check it out here: www.CultureCounter.app

Questions for "Culture Eats Strategy for Breakfast"

- Let's talk about that refrigerator email. Yikes. How did you feel after reading that?
- Talk about a moment you've shared or received a "refrigerator email"–type experience with others.
- What is culture?
- Who's responsible for building culture in your organization?
- Share some examples of how you have created or destroyed culture through your behavior toward others.
- Describe your company culture without mentioning perks and benefits. What would you change or adjust?
- Why do "Behaviors eat culture for lunch"?
- Consider Taj's driving style in India and his driving style in Houston. Where have you seen other examples of behaviors transforming because of the environment?
- Think about your own leadership journey. Tell a story about a leader who improved your organization's culture through their behavior. How did that make you feel?
- After reading this chapter, are you skeptical about behaviors creating or destroying culture? If so, share those thoughts with the group.
- What were some of your biggest takeaways or *ah-ha* moments from this chapter?
- Share a moment of self-awareness about your leadership after reading this chapter.
- What, if anything, will you change or adjust about how you lead or behave based on what you've read?

CHAPTER 3

Behavior Eats Culture for Lunch

Our pivot to Love as a Business Strategy didn't happen overnight. We still had plenty of kinks to work out, such as our laissez-faire approach to scheduling leadership meetings. We operated on "Moh Time": If Mohammad felt like he needed Moh Time™ with us, he'd send out an invite and expect us all to be there.

We also tended to show up late. During one meeting in particular, nobody showed up to Moh Time on time. One member of the leadership team ambled in a minute late, then another showed up a minute later, and then another leader a minute after that.

With each new arrival, Mohammad's face grew increasingly tense. He *hated* when people were late—and Frank *still* wasn't in his seat.

"What the hell is this?" Mohammad bellowed. "Frank is *never* on time for a single meeting. He has no sense of responsibility!"

The gathered team members looked around, confirmed that Frank was indeed missing, and shrugged.

Mohammad tried to bury his anger and start the meeting anyway, but after a frustrating few minutes, threw up his hands, stalked out of the conference room, and headed straight for Frank's office.

Mohammad burst into Frank's room to find him calmly sitting at his computer. "Why the <bleep> aren't you at the meeting?" he shouted. Frank turned around with a blank look on his face. Then Mohammad unleashed a flurry of words that we've elected not to put in print.

Frank blinked, tears filling his eyes. He mumbled an apology, then followed Mohammad to the conference room.

We didn't get much done in the meeting. With Mohammad shaking in anger and Frank looking utterly defeated in a corner, no one could focus on any work. Eventually, the conversation wrapped, and everyone went back to their desks.

That's when Mohammad began to reflect on what he had just done—and, more important, on what he *shouldn't* have done. Had he crossed a line?

Later that day, Mohammad's calendar pinged. It was an invite from Frank for a one-on-one meeting. . .in the quietest, most isolated meeting room in the entire office.

Oh crap, Mohammad thought. *Is Frank going to quit because of how I treated him?*

This wouldn't be the first time someone had quit over Mohammad's misbehavior, but he was trying to be better now. How could things go so sideways so quickly?

The next day, Mohammad was a few minutes late to the meeting, unable to settle his nerves. When he finally walked through the door, he found Frank calmly sitting at the table. In front of him were his notebook, his closed laptop, and nothing else.

Mohammad immediately sat down and recited a litany of excuses. He'd had a terrible day before the meeting. He hated it when no one showed up on time. He had a tight schedule and couldn't waste a second. All excuses, no apologies.

"Mohammad, may I speak?" Frank said.

"Sure, sure, sure!" Mohammad sputtered as he tried to calm down.

His hands shaking, Frank reached for his notebook and began to read. "I did not appreciate how I was treated yesterday. I did not appreciate the tone you used, the words you said, and the volume at which you said it. It made me feel disrespected and unsafe." Frank paused and took a deep breath. "I don't think that kind of behavior is what we're working so hard to create here."

Frank put the notebook down, his hands still shaking. A long silence followed.

Finally, Mohammad sighed. "You're right. I'm sorry. I apologize. That wasn't okay, and it won't happen again."

Mohammad was sincere in his apology, but would it be enough to stop Frank from resigning?

"There's one more thing I want to share with you." Frank opened up his laptop and showed him the calendar event Moh had created for the previous day's Moh Time. Mohammad scanned the list of invitees and realized his mistake: Frank hadn't been late to the leadership meeting. He'd never been invited in the first place.

"I had no idea what was going on," Frank said. "I only followed you into the meeting because I didn't want to lose my job."

"Frank, I'm so, so sorry," Mohammad said again, a fresh wave of shame washing over him.

So why hadn't Frank resigned? The thought had crossed his mind, but he chose to embrace the incident as a teaching opportunity instead. Frank had bought in fully to Mohammad's vision for a culture of love, and he knew he had a role to play in creating it. Regardless of how Mohammad responded, Frank had a responsibility to step up and tell Mohammad what his behavior had felt like from the other side.

That wasn't an easy responsibility to embrace. In fact, it was one of the most difficult professional conversations Frank had ever had. Confrontation is *not* in Frank's DNA. But, on the advice of one of Softway's VPs, Frank showed up prepared. He wrote down everything he wanted to say and how it had made him feel ahead of time and committed to being as cool and level-headed as he could possibly be.

It worked. Frank's bravery showed Mohammad the impact of his behaviors and taught us all a crucial lesson. As we said in Chapter 2, culture may eat strategy for breakfast, but behaviors eat culture for lunch.

Since the late 1990s, organizations have increasingly stressed the importance of culture in a thriving operation. Their hearts are in the right place, but their focus is unnecessarily broad, failing to account for the impact of individual behavior on culture as a whole.

Here's how it goes: Groups are made of individuals. Each day, those individuals behave in a way that either strengthens or destroys their relationships with others. And as their relationships go, so goes the organizational culture. The healthier the relationships, the healthier the culture. The more toxic those relationships, the more toxic the culture. It follows, then, that if a culture of love is the goal, our individual behaviors are the only path forward. A group cannot change if those within it are unwilling to change themselves.

So let's talk about our behavior—the good, the bad, and the ugly. This is a big conversation, so to help guide it we have broken behavior down into three categories:

1. **Mindsets:** The foundations of our behaviors
2. **Attitudes:** The outward expression of our mindsets
3. **Communication:** How we engage with others based on our mindset and attitude

In the first part of this chapter, we'll explore each of these categories and how they impact our behaviors at work. Then we'll wrap up the conversation by talking about what it looks like when everything goes wrong: misbehavior.

Mapping Mindsets

Every day you wake up with a perspective that orients your approach to life. That perspective is called a mindset. Mindsets don't just affect your home life or your work life; they affect everything. All attitudes, communication, and actions ultimately have their roots in your mindset—how you perceive the world.

In her book *Mindset: The New Psychology of Success*, author Carol Dweck outlined two distinct ways of viewing the world: fixed mindset and growth mindset.[1] In the next discussion, we're going to explore the key points of her argument. As you read, keep in mind that no one is entirely one thing or the other. While each of us defaults to one mindset or the other, we all bounce between the two through the course of our lives.

THE FIXED MINDSET

In a fixed mindset, you are closed off to new opportunities. This could manifest itself in a number of ways:

- **Fear:** You worry you can't complete a task or do your job properly, or you are unwilling to try new things because you don't think you are capable.
- **Guilt and shame:** A single failure overshadows previous successes.

- **Persecution:** Everything is a competition—just you against the world.
- **Scarcity:** You're threatened by others' success. The more they have and achieve, the less is available to you.
- **Judgment:** You're constantly judging others, and you feel constantly judged.
- **Inflexibility:** Once you have made a judgment about a person or a situation, that's forever how you will see it.

As you might have guessed, the fixed mindset is incompatible with a culture of love. By its nature, it can lead only to behaviors that aren't inclusive, empathetic, or loving.

THE GROWTH MINDSET

The growth mindset is adaptable and resilient. The more problems you face, the more opportunities you have to learn. Common beliefs of a growth-focused mindset include:

- **Learning is key:** It's not what you don't know. It's what you don't know *yet*. Every moment is an opportunity to grow and try new things.
- **Failure is temporary:** Failure is a beginning, not an end. New approaches to a problem will lead to success. If not, you will learn and grow from the experience.
- **Success is contagious:** When others succeed, you're inspired, encouraged, and ready to celebrate. Success is available to anyone, so there's no pressure to compete.
- **Strengths take priority:** You see others as intelligent, talented, resilient, and capable of learning and supporting others.
- **Vulnerability is strength:** You assume others are there to help you rather than hinder you. By sharing your concerns, fears, and mistakes, you create a space for others to do the same.

At risk of stating the obvious, a growth mindset is essential for creating a culture of love, boosting your chances of success, building resilience, and fostering an environment of learning. Without it, you may find that the attitudes you project don't align with the beliefs you hold.

Let's put these mindsets in the context of Mohammad and Frank's encounter. Mohammad's mindset at the outset of the meeting was fixed. He saw time as a scarce resource, he felt persecuted when others showed up late, and he judged everyone in the room (especially Frank) for the slights he perceived.

However, when Frank confronted him, Mohammad didn't *stay* in a fixed mindset. The moment he realized he was in the wrong, he switched from fixed to growth, allowed himself to become vulnerable, and asked for Frank's forgiveness. A fixed mindset, then, doesn't have to be, well, fixed.

We should also note that Mohammad wasn't doing this consciously. At the time, the concepts of fixed and growth mindsets weren't yet in our vocabulary. We only knew that misbehaviors such as yelling, blaming, and shaming were antithetical to our mission, and that we couldn't ignore our misbehavior if we were called out for it.

Mindset Is Contagious

Think about the team you work with. How do you respond to failure as a group? Do you throw up your hands in defeat, or do you bear down and get to work?

While it's impossible to know the deepest thoughts of every member of your team, normally you can guess their mindsets by observing their words and actions. Look for these cues whenever possible. After all, you can't change what you don't measure. Then, once you notice that a fixed mindset has begun to take hold, you can adjust your own thoughts and behaviors to positively influence those around you.

Addressing Attitudes

If your mindset represents the way you think, your attitude is the outward manifestation of that thinking. The way we see it, there are three essential attitudes: Flyer, Fighter, and Influencer. To understand how these attitudes might manifest, let's return to our opening vignette about Moh Time. As you will see, had Frank chosen to operate from a different mindset, it would have dramatically affected the outcome of their conversation.

THE FLYER

Flyers may have the power or authority to confront a situation, but instead they choose to avoid it, complain, or play the victim.

Imagine Mohammad has just burst into Frank's office, snapping him out of the bliss of his deep work session. After Mohammad laces into him for a while, Frank responds by making excuses about why he wasn't at the meeting.

"I didn't have the chance to check my emails."
"Jeff asked me to work on something super-urgent."
"Chris distracted me with a Beyoncé meme."

With each excuse and deflection, Frank the Flyer does whatever he can to deflect blame from himself and play the victim. Rather than confront the situation, he runs from it.

Of course, you know the real story, so you know that Frank really did have a valid reason for not being at the meeting—and that he didn't flee from Mohammad when confronted.

THE FIGHTER

Let's rewind the situation. Once again, Mohammad has just stormed into Frank's office and begun yelling at him. This time, Frank the Fighter is having none of it and immediately starts pushing back.

"What are you trying to say, Mohammad? That I'm lazy?" Frank sneers. Behind this tough-guy veneer, Frank is still afraid of looking bad. However, by leaning into the conflict, he distracts Mohammad from the core issue and therefore deflects any criticism.

And another way to deflect? Turn the tables. "Oh, like *you're* so great," Frank might say, "you can't even manage a consistent meeting schedule!" By pointing out the folly of Moh Time, Frank the Fighter hopes to look better by comparison.

THE INFLUENCER

Both the Flyer and the Fighter act out of fear—fear of being wrong, fear of being fired, fear of being publicly embarrassed, and so on.

In this way, the Flyer and the Fighter are both manifestations of a fixed mindset, focused on reacting rather than on learning. Once you become aware of Flyers' and Fighters' attitudes, you begin to see how common they are in a business setting—and how much they can impact organizational culture.

By contrast, our third attitude, the Influencer, arises from a growth mindset—and, we're proud to say, is the attitude the real Frank chose to embody. Confronted with a challenging situation, Frank sought out ways to support and teach others and to better himself. He sought feedback from other team members, and then he invited Mohammad to a calm, rational conversation. . .in the darkest corner of the office.

In choosing this path, Frank the Influencer saw this problem as an opportunity for growth and learning, which interested him far more than being right. In fact, even if he hadn't been in the right (which he was), he still could have chosen the path of the Influencer by embracing Mohammad's criticism, admitting he was wrong, asking for forgiveness, and committing to correcting his behavior. Easy peasy: no lost energy to drama, competition, and politics.

Are You a Flyer, Fighter, or Influencer?

Just as we can alternate between growth and fixed mindsets, we can also shift among the attitudes of Flyer, Fighter, and Influencer. In some situations, we respond with fear. In others, we respond with openness and curiosity. Often the reasons for our varied responses are unknown even to us. It could be that a particular situation triggers a strong flight response. Or it could be that a certain person, for whatever reason, stirs the fighter sleeping within.

To a degree, these responses are out of our control. We may think we're responding as an Influencer only to receive feedback to the contrary later on. As external manifestations of our mindset, attitudes aren't about how we perceive ourselves but how others perceive us—and it can be difficult to know what that looks like without help.

During our Culture Rise leadership events, we utilize an exercise to help attendees understand how others perceive their attitudes. First, each person is assigned an attitude. Then, when it's their turn, they act out an exaggerated version of that attitude in front of the group.

This exercise might sound straightforward, but many people struggle. Fighters struggle to be Flyers, Flyers struggle to be Influencers, Influencers struggle to be Fighters, and so on. The participant tries to portray one attitude, but the audience perceives another!

This exercise demonstrates an all-too-real dynamic in the workplace. Without feedback, many of us don't have a clear idea of how we behave at work. We may see ourselves as Influencers, while others see us as Fighters.

The next time you find yourself in an uncomfortable situation at work, take a moment afterward to assess your attitude. How did you see yourself in that moment? What did you do (or not do) that led you to feel that way? Do you think others perceived your attitude the same way? Why or why not?

Considering Communication

Still with us? Let's recap so far. Your mindset is something internal to you. No one else can see your thoughts or read your feelings. They can only see how your feelings manifest through your attitude, which is the form and manner in which your mindset expresses itself to others. Now let's add communication to the mix.

Both your mindsets and attitudes show themselves in how you communicate—which often can lead to mixed messages. For instance, you could have great intentions and yet still communicate in a way that leaves a bad taste in your teammates' mouths. Alternatively, you could have not-so-great intentions but communicate in a way that makes others feel good. In a culture of love, neither of these outcomes is ideal. Each represents a form of communication breakdown.

To understand what's going on in these moments, first let's start with the two core types of communication:

♦ **Intrapersonal:** This is internalized communication or communication within yourself. For instance, after Mohammad barged in on Frank and started yelling at him, Frank could have told himself the story that Mohammad was out to get him. The more Frank told himself this story, the more his relationship with Mohammad would have suffered.

◆ **Interpersonal:** This is communication between two or more people, whether verbally, in writing, or through body language—and often in combination. For instance, Mohammad could have said to Frank, "I think it's really wonderful that you weren't at the meeting on time today." However, if he was grinding his teeth and pacing around the room while he said it, Frank would rightfully interpret that statement as being sarcastic or otherwise insincere.

Successful communicators are mindful of how they communicate both intrapersonally and interpersonally. They're mindful of the stories they tell themselves and aligned in their mindset, attitudes, and communication so that they can communicate authentically with their team.

Naturally, in a culture of love, authentic communication is the goal—both because it leads to better results and because, well, inauthentic communication is hard to keep up. It's easy to think you can put on a mask and hide what you're feeling, but masks crack. Eventually, whether through verbal or nonverbal cues, people *will* see through the mask to what you really feel. Maybe your voice will crack. Maybe you'll catch yourself scowling when you meant to be smiling. Even if these cues last only a moment, those moments speak volumes.

Fortunately, authentic communication is just as plain to see—and in the long run, it requires far less energy. Why put in all that effort to maintain a cracking mask when you could just admit that you're upset and ask for a moment to calm down? Sure, taking a step back feels like the opposite of progress, but, in reality, it will get you further than pretending ever could.

Unforgiveness: The Root of all Misbehavior

Now that you understand how mindset, attitudes, and communication come together, let's bring this conversation back to the main topic of this chapter: behavior. When you behave constructively, you contribute to a culture of love. When you behave destructively, you strip away that culture.

We all misbehave sometimes. However, if we are to grow from these moments, then we must first understand the many different flavors of misbehavior and where they come from. While the next list is far from exhaustive, these are the misbehaviors you're likely to encounter (or exhibit) in the workplace:

◆ **Verbal attacks:** These were the old Mohammad's specialty, whether it was yelling in a meeting, cutting others off, or sending nasty-grams about refrigerator etiquette via email.

◆ **Emotional abuse:** These piercing statements cut deeper than verbal attacks by attempting to make the recipient feel dumb, slow, or incompetent. Emotional abuse usually is deployed to stop an argument dead in its tracks, often under the guise of "showing you how I feel" or "putting you in your place."

◆ **Apathy:** This misbehavior often manifests as some form of the silent treatment. You ignore a teammate by pulling out your phone, you actively avoid certain topics or conflicts, or you neglect to give a team member important feedback. In any case, you're not invested enough in the team's success to help it.

◆ **Disassociation:** This is the weaponized version of apathy. Instead of simply behaving indifferently, a disassociated person actively ignores others, refuses to give them work, or refuses to ask them for help—even if doing so is to the detriment of the project and the company.

◆ **Mind games:** We like to joke that the modern practitioner of mind games was the designer of complex torture devices in medieval times. At their core, mind games are overcomplicated and manipulative, designed to get something you want while avoiding any responsibility for the outcome. One common mind game is a concept known as gaslighting, whereby a person deliberately denies, misrepresents, or omits critical information in order to confuse another person into believing they're in the wrong. To a practitioner, mind games often feel like justice. But to those on the receiving end, they are anything but.

- ◆ **Financial repercussions:** In the workplace, financial repercussions could mean denying someone a promotion or pay
  increase. Or it could be more subtle, such as reducing a team
  or department budget as a way of getting back at someone.

Although all these misbehaviors manifest in different ways, they
all stem from the same root problem—what we call *unforgiveness.*

To illustrate what we mean, let's turn once again to the story of
the missed meeting. When Frank first confronted Mohammad about
his misbehavior, the first thing Mohammad did was blame other
people—in this case, leadership's tendency for being late to meetings. This is often the telltale sign of unforgiveness. It's never your
fault, but someone else's:

"I was stressed."
"Jeff made a mistake, so I had to do what I had to do."
"Chris tried to humiliate me."
"Yeah, I yelled at Frank, but it was to teach him a lesson."

We've all said things like this. And we all know that, deep down,
they're just excuses. Nevertheless, we find ourselves going to elaborate lengths to justify our misbehaviors—all because we couldn't find
it in our hearts to forgive someone (or often, to forgive ourselves).

Here's the thing about unforgiveness: It's most likely to rear its
head in the relationships we care most about. Why? Because those
relationships have history—and history is never just sunshine and
roses. Yes, familiarity really does breed contempt. We'll go out of our
way to apologize for bumping into a stranger on the street but yell at
a family member for doing the same thing. It's not that we love the
stranger more. It's that we have a lot of unresolved anger toward the
people we love, even if we don't mean or want to.

The same phenomenon happens in the workplace. Slowly over
time, we get into the habit of disregarding our close coworkers' feelings. Then, after the first perceived slight, we begin to take their
goodwill for granted and start allowing ourselves to misbehave. We
may write this off as innocent, but it's not. The more familiar we are
with another person, the better able we are to hurt them. With each
misbehavior, with each act of unforgiveness, we chip away at our
culture until there's nothing left.

What's Your Favorite Way to Misbehave?

During our Culture Rise leadership experiences, we ask participants to choose which misbehaviors they default to. Many pick apathy or disassociation. When things get hairy, they simply disconnect. Participants are far less likely to admit to verbal attacks, emotional abuse, or mind games—even though, if you look at any workplace, these misbehaviors are just as common as any other.

As you consider your own go-to misbehaviors, you're likely to find two answers: the misbehavior you want to do, and the misbehavior you actually do. We often deny the former and focus only on the latter, but with a little digging, you can get at the truth.

For instance, many participants who choose apathy often do so because they ignore coworkers they don't like. Fair, but ignoring someone is also a sign you're playing mind games. To determine the true misbehavior, ask yourself a follow-up question: Does it matter to you if the person notices? If no, then your go-to misbehavior really is apathy. If yes—and especially if you change tactics afterward—then your real favorite misbehavior is mind games.

It's not easy facing down our own petty sides. (We know from experience. Just ask Mohammad how thrilled he is to see so many of his own misbehaviors in print!) However, once you understand this side of yourself, you're in a position to contextualize and come to terms with them.

In the early stages of understanding, you will be tempted to associate misbehavior with an external trigger. Someone else was incompetent. Someone else scared you or pushed you out of control. However, dig deeper into your own reactions. You'll nearly always find unforgiveness at the root.

Introducing Introspection

Here, at the end of Part I, you should have a good understanding of what love looks like in a business sense, how love is ultimately expressed through culture, and how culture is the sum total of individual behaviors. Further, you should understand the mindsets, attitudes, and communication patterns that inform our behavior. You should also have a good grasp of what misbehaviors look like and what triggers them. Now that you understand all the components that contribute to a culture of love, you can begin to rethink your own behaviors with clarity and intention—and, in so doing, help bring love to your workplace.

In Part II, you'll take this process of transformation one step further through our Six Pillars of Love. But before we get started, there's one last piece of the behavior puzzle we want to address: introspection.

In business, we're more accustomed to reflection than true introspection. We might reflect on a meeting we had, our department goals for the quarter, or the year's fiscal results. Often these moments of reflection are framed in terms of performance: What did we do well? What could we have done better?

Reflection is useful, but it's only a surface-level assessment. After Mohammad yelled at Frank over the alleged missed meeting, he reflected on his behavior and concluded he had misbehaved. However, it wasn't until after Frank confronted him that he thought to look within himself and understand the *reasons* he had misbehaved. *Why* did he get angry? *Why* did he think it was okay to treat Frank the way he had? Questions like these are the work not of reflection, but of introspection.

Introspection means thoughtfully assessing where you are, what needs to change, and why. Such a process is naturally time-consuming—which is why most of us default to reflection. That said, introspection is essential to building a culture of love. If you really want to change your behavior, you must understand why you behave the way you do and, more important, what you can do differently.

Effective introspection requires a few key components:

◆ **Gather feedback:** You can't rely on someone like Frank to book a one-on-one with you every time you misbehave. You can, however, connect with others to learn from your experiences, work on uncovering your true motivations, and understand the root causes of your behaviors. From there, you can work on corrective actions that will yield meaningful results.

- **Consistency:** Introspection isn't easy to maintain. It requires a prolonged focus on your own motivations and actions. If you start by considering why you got angry, but then you veer off into thoughts about how no one shows up to your meetings on time, you've lost the thread. You are blaming rather than introspecting. Maintain the focus on yourself and don't get distracted by other factors.

- **Accountability:** It's easy to say you're a good person and that as long as you have good intent, nothing else matters. In reality, intent doesn't matter. People can't see intent. Actions will drive how other people perceive you. Don't allow intent to become a get-out-of-jail-free card. Focus on what happened, why it happened, and what you can do about it either now or next time a similar situation arises.

- **Patience:** Many people put off the work of introspection because they feel as if the process never ends. They're right: It doesn't. However, while the work of introspection may never end, it does come much easier with practice.

If there's one thing you take from this chapter, it's the importance of introspection. No attempt to grow a culture of love will happen as quickly or as well without first cultivating this ability. You can't control a lot in this world, but you *can* control yourself and your behaviors.

Is any of this easy? Absolutely not. Often the act of introspection might bring up painful memories from your past that you'd just as soon prefer to leave buried. If you're not ready to go that deep, then you don't have to. Every little insight, however small, is still useful not just in your work life, but in your whole life.

But however far you're willing to go, do the work. Don't let yourself off the hook. The only way to create a culture of love is the hard way. If you can commit to the process—if you can commit to *yourself*—then you will have unlocked all the tools you need to make it a reality.

Building Self-Awareness

Ignoring your emotions, your triggers, and your patterns won't make them any easier to deal with. It just makes you look as if you blew up for no reason. Better by far to welcome humanity back into the workplace and deal with reality than to confuse and alienate your teammates.

For more resources to help you practice introspection, please visit www.LoveAsAStrategy.com/resources.

Questions for "Behavior Eats Culture for Lunch"

- ◆ Let's talk about Mohammad's outburst toward Frank about him "missing" that meeting. If you were Frank in that situation, how would you have reacted?
- ◆ When it comes to fixed or growth mindsets, which do you most frequently default to with coworkers? Why?
- ◆ Share a story about your mindset shifting from a fixed mindset to a growth mindset at work. What caused this change?
- ◆ After reading through the three attitudes (Flyer, Fighter, Influential), which one of these attitudes do you see commonly showcased at your workplace?
- ◆ Unforgiveness is rarely addressed in the workplace—why don't we talk about the need for forgiveness/grace at work?
- ◆ If we're honest with ourselves, we have misbehaved at work. Considering the misbehaviors outlined in this chapter, which one resonates with you?
- ◆ Which misbehavior do you experience from others most often at work?
- ◆ What is the impact on culture (the behavior of your team) when they experience that type of misbehavior at work?
- ◆ Share an example of your misbehavior (at work) with the group.
- ◆ How has unforgiveness toward others contributed to your misbehavior?

- What are some ways you've begun to introspect on your behavior (or misbehavior) toward others?
- How has introspection helped you realize moments where you misbehave with others?
- After reading this chapter, are you skeptical about whether misbehavior or unforgiveness negatively impacts your workplace? If so, share those thoughts with the group.
- What were some of your biggest takeaways or *ah-ha* moments from this chapter?
- How have you begun to build better self-awareness around your behaviors?

Closing Out Part I

- What was the most surprising part of Mohammad's transformation story?
- What stories in Part I resonated with you the most? Why?
- What's holding you back from fully embracing love in your workplace?
- What lessons from Part I are you going to start incorporating in the way you lead others?
- How are you contributing to the culture of the organization?
- What behaviors (or misbehaviors) do you experience most often in your workplace?

Note

1. Carol Dweck, *Mindset: The New Psychology of Success* (New York: Ballantine, 2007).

PART II

Understanding the Culture of Love

By now you have a good understanding of what a culture of love is and how individual behaviors can either create or destroy it. Here in Part II, we're going to start building on top of that foundation with what we call the *Six Pillars of Love*.

As you move through these chapters, keep in mind two things:

First, while we've laid these pillars out in a specific order, in practice they are interrelated and interdependent. Inclusion, for instance, depends on trust, empathy, and vulnerability to succeed.

In that way, these pillars are much like the cylinders of an engine. You need all six firing in harmony to create momentum and move forward. If even one cylinder is firing out of sync, performance suffers—and the engine might fail.

Second, these pillars all represent words and concepts you've heard before. You might even be tired of hearing them. We understand, but we also ask you to keep an open mind. We approach the pillars of inclusion, empathy, vulnerability, trust, empowerment, and forgiveness through a practitioner's lens, driven by our lived experiences, mistakes, and triumphs. The value is not in the concept but in the practice.

To that end, as you read these stories ask yourself: How can I apply this pillar to myself? What would this look like in my organization? Through these questions, you might discover that some of these pillars are quite strong in your organization—and that some are missing entirely.

45

CHAPTER 4

Inclusion

Imagine feeling like you don't have a voice at your work. Imagine feeling belittled and small, disengaged from your job and pushed aside. Now imagine literally traveling to the other side of the world—enduring nearly twenty-four hours of flights and layovers—just to feel that way.

Until 2016, this is exactly how our Indian teammates felt when they traveled to Houston. We know because they have told us. Unfortunately, it took us far too long to ask for and learn from that feedback.

In fact, this issue wasn't even on our radar until the first time Chris traveled to India. From almost the moment he arrived, Chris was struck by how his Indian teammates went out of their way to accommodate him. They picked him up from the airport. They took him shopping for groceries and essentials. They took him out to dinner. They even cleared their weekends just so they could show Chris the sights and sounds of Bengaluru. When he first set foot in Softway's Indian office, one of his fellow teammates even offered Chris his lunch—practically forcing it into his hands as he walked toward a meeting!

Chris loved feeling welcomed and included, and he appreciated his teammates for the effort. But the more he had time to reflect on the experience, the more he realized that this amazing treatment extended only in one direction.

By contrast, we hadn't considered our team members' experience during their short-term visits to the United States at all. We thought only of ourselves and our own needs. Sometimes someone on our Houston team would offer a visiting team member a lift from the airport, and sometimes they wouldn't. There were no grocery runs, no dinners, no weekend fun, and definitely no team members eager to offer up their lunch. As a result, these teammates felt alone, isolated, and ignored—which was antithetical to a culture of love.

Once Chris understood the problem, he knew it needed to stop.

Unsure how to begin, Chris reached out to a few Indian team members to learn firsthand what their visits to Houston had been like. To Chris's surprise, many of the visitors reported having difficulty sleeping their first night in town. Why? Nerves. Many of these team members had waited their whole lives to visit America. The opportunity was thrilling. . .and not at all conducive to getting a good night's sleep.

That initial excitement, however, usually gave way to a different feeling: isolation. Outside of work, these team members had to figure out everything on their own—where to eat, where to get basic supplies, and even where to get a haircut. At work, they were mostly ignored, often spending meals and breaks by themselves in a corner of the break room. They felt alone and voiceless.

To correct this, Chris implemented several new policies.

First, Softway began creating welcome baskets for all visiting team members—complete with a towel, a mug, and some of their favorite chai and Flaming Hot Cheetos. (Yes, really. More on those later.) The baskets were then capped off with a series of personalized welcome notes handwritten by US employees. These welcome baskets were the first thing visiting team members would see when they entered our company apartment, allowing us to make early connections with them and give them a few conversation starters for their first in-person meetings the next day.

Second, Chris made sure that a Softway team member would always be at the airport to offer a ride, take our visitor out to dinner (or pick it up if they were too tired), and help them stock the apartment for their visit.

Finally, Chris initiated a company policy that Houston team members make time to show their counterparts around—whether that's taking them out to a nice Cajun dinner, inviting them to a Beyoncé concert, or taking them to a local monument.

All of this might sound like a lot of work. It is. But it's the least we can do to make every team member feel welcome, valued, and included. That's what the first of our Six Pillars of Love is all about: making sure that everyone in your organization has what they need to speak, contribute, and show up fully to work. Both inclusion and its antecedent, marginalization, are nuanced, tricky subjects. Approached haphazardly, efforts to address them can be ineffective at best and actively damaging at worst. Here's how we work to navigate unpredictable waters.

Why Inclusion Matters

In organizations that don't explicitly emphasize inclusion, many team members feel as if aspects of who they are might not be welcome or appreciated. Feeling excluded, they hold back important parts of themselves that could potentially add value to the organization.

A culture rooted in inclusion enables everyone to contribute at a high level, leading to more productive teams that produce better organizational outcomes. However, this doesn't happen by default. Organizations must look for opportunities to include everyone—and to encourage others to do the same—even when it's more convenient and less costly not to.

It took zero effort for us to ignore our visiting Indian team members. Picking them up from the airport, creating welcome baskets, and showing them the local culture, in contrast, take a lot of effort. But it's precisely this effort that makes inclusion so valuable: It tells our team members that they matter to us and that we have taken their needs into account. If that means taking a little extra time out of our days to accommodate them, so be it. In a culture of love, the alternative is not an option.

Inclusion and belonging are basic human needs. When we meet that need at work, we create a better world in microcosm. For that reason alone, inclusion is worth it. However, executed consistently and effectively, inclusion also leads to better organizational outcomes—better innovation and creativity, greater empathy, more employee retention, and increased resilience. It invites more diverse voices to the table and gives those voices permission and comfort to speak. Finally, it creates a greater sense of loyalty and belonging, enabling both individuals and teams to flourish.

The Difference Between Diversity and Inclusion

The term *diversity, equity,* and *inclusion* (commonly referred to as DEI) has become a big (and sometimes controversial) buzzword in the corporate lexicon. But while many organizations emphasize DEI, far fewer are able to point to tangible results from their efforts.

Why is this? One reason is intention. DEI training and hiring practices are often undertaken for the wrong reasons—specifically, to avoid lawsuits. Unfortunately, when DEI is only code for CYA (a cheeky industry abbreviation for "cover your ass"), then any training or recruiting efforts intended to address this issue often create more bias than they solve.

While diverse hiring practices are important, all the diverse hires in the world will not benefit your organization if you're not making a sincere effort to make everyone on your team feel like they belong.

We practice DEI through direct action. We address this by representing people of different backgrounds and different levels of seniority in key meetings. In so doing, we recognize and acknowledge our need to hear from divergent thinkers or those with unique perspectives. Otherwise, why would we have put so much emphasis on hiring them in the first place?

Of course, we're a work in progress just like anyone else. Even an organization with good intentions might not realize that their hiring, promotion, and growth practices are inherently biased in how they are applied. To create lasting change, leaders must be willing to carefully examine their own behaviors and attitudes, as well as how they design every process and system. Without addressing these biases, no number of new hires or workshops will solve the problem; the situation will only perpetuate itself.

For more diversity, equity, and inclusion resources, including a free, exhaustive DEI glossary, visit www.LoveAsAStrategy.com/resources.

The Many Faces of Marginalization

Have you ever been excluded? Were you ever not invited to a party when everyone else was? How did that feel?

A marginalized workforce is extremely damaging to organizational outcomes—especially because it's a problem that often goes unnoticed. We certainly weren't aware that we were marginalizing our Indian team members, but that thoughtlessness created lasting damage to our organization that took us quite a while to repair. Eventually, we understood that a culture of love means actively recognizing and attending to the needs and experiences of others.

Conversations around marginalization usually center around race, but beliefs surrounding a person's gender, religion, or ability could also be factors, as well as their job title, wealth, or social status. In fact, whether due to these or other factors, we've all felt excluded or marginalized at different points in our lives—and in both large and small ways.

In order to have discussions around diversity, equity, and inclusion without focusing on any one criterion, it is important to understand the concept of dominant and nondominant groups. Here's the gist: Regardless of where you are or what room you enter, some people will have a lot in common and some won't. The former is the dominant group, while the latter is the nondominant group.

These differences can be subtle, especially when obvious similarities exist between both groups. For instance, picture a room full of white men. All of them are married, have two kids, and root for the Packers. However, their educational profiles are different; 80 percent of the men went to a private university, while the remaining 20 percent did not.

This may not sound like a meaningful difference, but it can influence many of the group's conversations. As a result, every time a member of the dominant group shares a story from their private university days, 20 percent of the room is reminded of their otherness. To be clear, this doesn't make the dominant group bad people. They're probably not even aware that they're excluding anyone. But even unintentional behavior can create the experience of excluding others. If this dynamic is left unchecked, it could lead members of the nondominant group to feel like second-tier, or otherwise unequal, team members.

As this example demonstrates, marginalization can happen to anyone for nearly any reason. Anyone can feel marginalized, and anyone can marginalize. Some marginalizations are small, and some are really big. Both can be harmful. In the next sections, we'll offer a few examples to help you better understand the many faces of marginalization.

CAN'T YOU JUST MAKE DO WITH THESE SCISSORS?

When Frank was fourteen, his dad gave him a new watch for his birthday. He was so excited, he put it on immediately and wore it to school the next day.

Then the kids started asking questions. "Why are you wearing your watch like that? You've got it on the wrong arm."

But Frank didn't have his watch on the wrong arm. He had it on his right arm—his nondominant arm—just as he had been taught to do. His classmates just weren't used to seeing a left-handed person wearing a watch.

If you're part of the 90 percent of the population that is right-handed, you may not think that being left-handed is a big deal. But then again, you'd have no reason to notice—the world is literally built for you.

For Frank and other left-handed people, however, navigating a right-handed world is a series of constant compromises and inconveniences. When they write, the text on the pen is upside down, the spine in the notebook gets in their way, and their hand smudges the ink as they move from left to right. If someone is a guitarist or a golfer, their options for testing out equipment before buying it are either limited or nonexistent. There's more: Tape measures are upside down, ergonomic scissors aren't so ergonomic, and can openers are more like *can't* openers.

Frank has also found that his left-handedness can lead to cultural misunderstandings. For instance, in India, your right hand is for eating, and your left hand is for wiping after you've relieved yourself. Frank was aware of this cultural norm before his first visit to India, so he went to great lengths to learn how to eat with his right hand. For the most part, he adapted. But every now and then, he would slip up, grab some food with his left hand, and endure dirty looks.

The experience of being left-handed can feel like death by a thousand papercuts. Like all left-handers, Frank is able to get through his day just fine. He's even able to have a sense of humor and/or play mind games about it. (Ask him about his "left-handers only" coffee mug that is designed to spill if a righty picks it up.). However, being left-handed in a right-handed world means enduring constant, daily inconveniences. There's not a day that goes by that people like Frank don't notice that the world wasn't built for them and that they're expected to accommodate the dominant group.

ONE STRIKE AGAINST YOU

When Chris was growing up, his mom gave him and his sister a warning: Chris already had one strike against him because he was Black, and his sister already had two strikes against her because she was both Black and a woman. Then, after explaining the challenges her children would face, Chris's mother would end the conversation with a question:

> "How many strikes are you going to add before someone takes you out?"

It wasn't an easy thing for Chris and his sister to hear—and it certainly wasn't an easy thing for Chris's mother to say—but she had resolved to prepare her children for an unforgiving world. In many ways, Chris thinks his mother did the right thing. All throughout his formative years, Chris knew that he couldn't afford to make the same mistakes as his peers. The world didn't work the same for people like him—both because he was Black and because his family didn't enjoy high socioeconomic status.

As a result, Chris did what many in marginalized or underrepresented groups do: He tried to find acceptance through assimilation and overcorrection. As Chris saw it, he didn't have the same margin for error that those in more dominant groups had. He typically felt the need to go along to get along. Acceptance is a basic human need, but Chris often felt that he had to work harder to get it.

Chris has gained this acceptance, but it has taken a bit of a trade-off to get there. For instance, when someone asks him to share a moment where he has made a mistake—such as yelling at a team-mate or blowing off work—he is often unsure what to say. He doesn't have stories like that because he never felt as if he had access to misbehavior the way those in more dominant groups do. The result is that Chris comes off as a perfectionist, as someone unwilling to be vulnerable and admit to past mistakes. To some, that's reason enough for another strike against him.

THE CHALLENGES OF BEING MUSLIM IN AN AIRPORT

Mohammad is a first-generation immigrant. He was born in Saudi Arabia to Indian parents and moved to the United States when he was sixteen. He is also a practicing Muslim American and is married to a Russian immigrant. With such a diverse background, Mohammad is judged in different places for different reasons. In India, he is judged for not being Hindu. In America, he is judged for appearing foreign, even though America (specifically Texas, which is like double America) has been his home for decades. In Europe, he is all but ignored by restaurant and hotel staff when he dresses casually—but when he dresses like a successful businessman, he is given the royal treatment.

There is one place, however, where Mohammad has always been treated the same: airports.

Since the events of September 11, 2001, air travel hasn't been easy for Mohammad. No matter what airport he's in, no matter where he's been or where he's headed, the experience is strikingly similar. First, airlines don't let him check in early online. When he arrives to check in, his reservation usually has a hold on it—though the agents never seem to know why. Then he has to stand around awkwardly for an extra ten to fifteen minutes while the agents not-so-discreetly run a security check.

If that was the extent of his problems, that would still be too much. But it's just the beginning. Mohammad is routinely pulled out of the Security and Immigration line for a secondary investigation. Often he's pulled out of line right in front of clients, coworkers, or even family, and then he is escorted to a private security room.

Once in these secondary rooms, Mohammad is separated from all his personal belongings—no passport, no phone, no luggage. Sometimes he is asked to remove his clothes and given a full body search, presumably to see if he has any explosives or weapons on him. Then he is asked a series of questions. "What business are you in?" "Why do you travel?" "What car do you drive?" "Do you have a chemical engineering degree?" Finally, after two or three hours in these glorified holding cells, security thanks him for his cooperation, escorts him out, and tells him to have a nice day.

Two or three hours is a long time to wait. Sometimes Mohammad is detained ahead of departure, in which case he usually misses his flight. Other times he is detained after landing, at which point he is tired, hungry, and thirsty from travel. Meanwhile, someone is usually waiting for him outside these holding areas—whether it's his wife and children, another Softway team member, or a client.

During one such incident, Mohammad was passing through New York on his way home from China. He had just been on a flight for fourteen hours and had already been waiting in a holding room for over two and half hours—which caused him to miss his connecting flight. And yet, when he asked for some water, the security officer told him to go drink out of the toilet, further dehumanizing him.

Nothing about Mohammad's treatment was normal. And yet, with no other choice but to comply, he began to alter his own behaviors—arriving three hours early or more—just so he could make his flights on time. But while he could adjust his behaviors so his marginalization didn't inconvenience him as much, he couldn't do anything to change the fact that he was being marginalized and dehumanized. Such treatment is profoundly wrong, no matter who is experiencing it, or why.

You Have Felt Different Too

You may not be left-handed, Black, or an Indian Muslim. But you don't have to be left-handed to understand what it feels like to be marginalized as a left-handed person. You don't need to be Black to understand what it feels like to be marginalized as a Black person. You don't have to be Muslim to understand what it feels like to be marginalized as a Muslim. At some point, in some way, and no matter who you are, you have walked into a room and been treated differently too.

When considering issues of marginalization, remember that feeling. Use it to inform how you relate to others and how you work to include them.

Inclusion is about more than giving everyone a welcome basket during a business trip. It's about more than just rooting out marginalization in all its forms. It's about making people feel welcomed. When people feel welcomed, they feel loved. It's about inviting new team members into the group, making space for their voice during meetings, and handling conflict with grace when it arises. While the work of inclusion isn't accomplished in a day, here are some tips and mindsets to help you along your way.

- Understand and accept that differences *do* exist between you and your teammates. Not everyone grows up and experiences life in the same way. Even if you don't know or understand the differences between yourself and a teammate, you *can* understand that differences exist—and that they could bring value and insight that might help your team achieve certain goals.
- Practice patience. It's not easy to make room for others whose experiences you don't fully understand. Conflicts, disagreements, and differences are inevitable—but that doesn't mean they need to kill conversation. Embrace the notion that differences are *bridges*, not gaps.
- Practice vulnerability. (See Chapter 6 for how.) Pride, arrogance, and self-importance are antithetical to a culture of love.
- Be an advocate. Inclusion is not passive. Don't just give people a seat at the table; make sure they are heard as well. Elevate the voices of the unheard or the not-included. Root out instances of marginalization. Create an environment where your coworkers can use their authority, power, and influence.

By amplifying and validating the contributions of others who might not otherwise be heard, you not only reinforce the idea that they are welcome and valued, but you help your team develop and vet a broader range of ideas from which to consider and act. This will lead to more discussions, more pushback, and sometimes more conflict. Great. That's the point. Creating space to hear more voices might require more patience in the moment, but, in the long run, it also lessens the risk of toxic groupthink. More perspectives allow for more wisdom.

Self-Awareness Is the Key to Inclusion

When you're in the dominant group, you're often not aware of it. Because you experience very little friction, you aren't aware of the friction that others in a nondominant group may be experiencing. But if that's the case, how do you become more aware of others' experiences and challenges?

Once again, the key is to practice introspection. Here are two questions you can ask yourself.

1. Who is silent? When the whole group gets together, who is the quietest? By nature, the dominant group is usually the loudest. By identifying the people who aren't speaking up as frequently (if at all), you can work to include them in the group.
2. Whom don't you know on your team? Usually, if you're part of a dominant group, then you likely feel connected to the other members of that group and have solid relationships with them. Therefore, if there is someone you don't know as well, it's probably because they don't share certain traits that you share with the rest of your team.

Once you have a better understanding of who might be feeling marginalized, get active. Have conversations. Use empathy. Pay attention to your team members' individual needs and ask how you can serve them so that you do not accidentally make a situation worse.

Be the Ally

Orienting yourself and your organization around the pillar of inclusion is hard. After all, realizing the problem is only half the battle. Unless you take direct action to solve an instance of marginalization, the problem will only remain—and often grow worse.

To show what we mean, let's return to the opening story of this chapter. Once Chris realized the problem of how our Indian team members were being treated upon arriving in Houston, he had to take several steps to address the issue. First and foremost, he had to help others understand that a problem existed and that it had to be addressed.

Unfortunately, when Chris first brought up the issue to Mohammad, he pushed back. Softway wasn't treating its Indian team members any differently than any other company would. Why should they go out of their way to change?

The two went back and forth on the issue, with Chris making little headway. Finally, seeing no other option, Chris said he would take on the responsibility himself.

That's when something finally clicked for Mohammad. Seeing Chris willing to step up and sacrifice his own personal time made Mohammad understand how strongly Chris felt—and how important the issue really was. Chris wasn't suggesting these changes simply because they were nice things to do. He was trying to correct an injustice that actively hurt their team members. He couldn't turn a blind eye any longer.

Righting the wrongs of marginalization isn't easy. When confronted with an instance of injustice, it is far easier to ignore it, downplay it, or say the harm was unintentional. In this case, intention is irrelevant. After all, no one intends to cause a car accident, but they're accountable for the impact and the aftermath all the same.

To practice inclusion, be an ally. Be the voice for those who need to be heard. Acknowledge your harm, and the harm of the organization, and ask yourself how you can be better. And above all, take responsibility for your own actions and behaviors.

Questions for "Inclusion"

+ Why are left-handed folks way more epic than right-handed folks? (Frank's "left-hander" contribution.)

+ Share an experience where you've felt marginalized (excluded) at work. How did that make you feel?

+ Describe how it feels to truly belong at work. How do you show up when you experience true belonging?

+ Consider your workplace—where do you think your organization could be marginalizing people unintentionally?

- In what situations (at work) are you reminded of your otherness?
- What are some ways you can personally start to make others on your team/in your organization feel more cared for?
- How can you help create space for people who don't have a voice or a seat at the table?
- Thinking practically, what are some simple ways to help people experience belonging in your workplace?
- In what ways can lack of self-awareness damage culture within your organization?
- Which story from this chapter resonated with you the most? Explain why.
- After reading this chapter, are you skeptical about the topics of marginalization, inclusion, and belonging in the workplace? If so, share those thoughts with the group.
- What were some of your biggest takeaways or *ah-ha* moments from this chapter?
- Share a moment of self-awareness about your leadership after reading this chapter.
- What, if anything, will change you or adjust about how you lead or behave based on what you've read? If so, share an example of something you might change.

CHAPTER 5

Empathy

Before joining Softway, Chris had never worked for a company with over half its team members on another continent. At first, interacting with his Indian coworkers over the phone felt strange and new. He couldn't see their faces and had trouble getting a feel for who they were as people. As a result, he found it difficult to fully commit to their interactions. So, when he began traveling to India to meet his teammates in person, he was grateful for the opportunity.

During one such trip, Chris had traveled to India with Mohammad. This was a big trip, jam-packed with things to do, meetings to attend, and decisions to make. As busy as his almost twenty-hour days were, Chris soon discovered a problem brewing that was far more urgent than anything else on the trip.

One morning before a meeting, Sunil, an HR manager, approached Chris and asked if he could speak with him one-on-one.

"I'm about to step into this meeting, Sunil. Is it urgent?" Chris said.

"Yes," Sunil said. "I *really* need to talk to you today."

Chris could tell Sunil was both desperate and frustrated. So, he agreed to bow out of the meeting and hear what his coworker had to say.

As soon as they found a quiet room to talk, the floodgates opened. Sunil oversaw the HR team in India and had been trying as hard as he could to do right by the company. However, in the eyes of his hiring managers, neither he nor his team was succeeding.

They weren't interested in Sunil's reasons why. They just wanted Sunil and his team to try harder. Faced with an impossible task, Sunil felt like everyone had given up on him—leaders and his peers alike.

Essentially, Sunil had two competing jobs. One job required monitoring employee attendance and tracking down any team member who didn't arrive to the office on time. (During this period, Softway was using biometric scanners to monitor employee movement; see Chapter 13.). It usually took Sunil and his team all morning to call every single late team member and file a report on their whereabouts. This meant that Sunil and his team had no time to perform their primary job: recruiting new candidates. As a result, every day when Sunil came to his afternoon status meeting, he was forced to report that his team was well behind on its quota.

Sunil and his team were locked in a vicious cycle. Every day they yelled at late employees. Every afternoon their managers yelled at them. Clearly, the system had set Sunil and his team up to fail. Something had to give—and soon—or Sunil worried his team would leave Softway for greener pastures.

Chris thanked Sunil for sharing and immediately went and found Mohammad.

"We need to talk *now*," Chris said.

For the next several minutes, Chris shared everything he'd heard. Using the pillar of empathy, here's how Chris and Mohammad tackled this problem head-on.

Jump in the Hole

There's an old adage that to understand a person, you must walk a mile in their shoes. Until we do, we often struggle to understand and embrace another person's experience. It is for this reason that practicing empathy may be the most challenging of the pillars of love—and also the most critical.

So what is empathy? As one of our colleagues says, "Empathy is being able to turn off your mic and turn up the volume on everyone else." In other words, empathy isn't just about understanding a problem; it's about understanding the underlying emotional experience. Then, with that shared perspective established, empathy is about moving forward together with someone rather than leaving them to struggle on their own.

In a culture of love, we've found that empathy is best understood through a concept known as *empathetic leadership*. We'll explain what that means in a moment. But to get there, first we need to draw a little contrast and show you what leadership—or, should we say *management*—looks like without empathy.

> Empathy means understanding and sharing the emotional experience that someone else is having—and then moving forward with that person to help resolve it.

THE APATHETIC MANAGER

Imagine you've just fallen into a big hole. After you spend a few minutes shouting for help, eventually someone comes along.

"What are you doing down in that hole?" the person says. "Get out—there's work to do!"

This is essentially what Sunil's managers were saying to him every time he spent the morning putting out fires involving absentee employees. Indifferent to his situation, Sunil's managers refused to see that Sunil and his team were struggling, and so they did little to help them.

By focusing only on outcomes, Sunil's managers effectively ignored his humanity, demanded that he put his feelings aside, and left him to fend for himself. They didn't do this to be cruel. They just thought that's how business was done.

Not in a culture of love. This approach might have worked in the short term, but, as Sunil made all too clear to Chris, in the long term it had only led to much bigger problems within the organization.

THE SYMPATHETIC MANAGER

New scenario: You're still in the hole, and you're still trying to figure a way out. Once again, someone comes along and sees your predicament.

"I'm so sorry you're in that hole," this new person says. "That must be terrible!"

Then they too continue on their way.

Well, they were nice, you think to yourself. But the result is the same. You're still in the hole.

This is the inherent challenge of working with a sympathetic manager. Sure, they mean well, but they rarely offer support in a way that empowers team members and furthers personal and professional growth.

Typically, the sympathetic manager responds to their team members' problems in one of two ways:

1. **The overhelpful approach.** Any time a manager pulls you off a job to take the burden off you, that's the overhelpful approach in action. Sure, their intentions are good, but instead of creating opportunities for growth, the sympathetic manager just redistributes the burden to others.

2. **The hands-tied approach.** "I'm sorry that's happening to you," the sympathetic manager might say, "but there's nothing I can do to help." Again, points for the kind words, but you're still stuck in a hole.

Chris almost took the hands-tied approach with Sunil. He was horrified by what he heard but uncertain of what he could do. If all Chris had done was listen, Sunil would have felt a degree of psychological safety, but Chris would have accomplished little else. The HR nightmare would still exist, and Sunil and his team would be no better off than they were before. Fortunately, as we'll see in the next section, Chris *didn't* stop there.

THE EMPATHETIC LEADER

Okay, one more time. You're still in the hole, and things still aren't going well. Again, someone walks by. But this time, the moment this person sees your predicament, they jump into the hole with you.

"All right," the person says, "let's get out of here. How can I help?"

That's empathetic leadership in action.

Throughout this discussion, you may have noticed that we've been careful to distinguish between the terms *manager* and *leader*. While these terms are often used interchangeably, to us their respective meanings are worlds apart.

Managers are people with formal authority and position at any level of an organization. They oversee other team members, but they don't lead them. Leaders, in contrast, serve their team members by supporting, mentoring, coaching, and otherwise setting their teams up for success. Leadership is learned—and ultimately earned—on the job. A leader earns the title not through a formal promotion but through the buy-in of their fellow team members.

Chris had to practice both vulnerability (see Chapter 6) and empathetic leadership to successfully address Sunil's concerns. First, he brought Mohammad into the conversation, putting him face-to-face with Sunil so that he could also hear Sunil's story firsthand. Doing this not only brought visibility to the issue, but it allowed Mohammad to make the same empathetic connection that Chris had. Then Chris and Mohammad resolved to change HR's approach to recruiting—specifically, to eliminate arbitrary quotas. Finally, over the next several weeks, they designed new training for the management team in India, so that management would be more aligned with their team members and be better able to reach their target outcomes.

The result? Recruiting was completely overhauled, Sunil could enjoy work again, and Softway became more effective at recruiting and retention. But more important, Chris's display of empathy created an unshakable bond among him, Sunil, and the company at large. As Sunil, who is still with the company, told us as we interviewed him for this story, "Everything good about me I learned at Softway and everything bad about me is just me."

What a difference.

> Apathetic management takes care of the business while disregarding the person. Sympathetic management takes care of the person while disregarding the business. Empathetic leadership takes care of the person in the context of the business.

The Key Traits of Empathy

To become an empathetic leader, the most important requirement is emotional intelligence. Emotional intelligence means being able to read the situation, assume good intent no matter how others are behaving, and connect your own experience to theirs in a way that leads to understanding. Here are two ways to actively build your emotional intelligence, whether at home or at work.

EMPATHETIC LISTENING

Empathetic listening is the practice of tuning everything else out and focusing directly on the other person. By listening to what the person is actually saying, rather than hearing only what you want to hear, you can respond to that person's needs productively.

Empathetic listening takes practice. It can be difficult to simultaneously hear what the person is saying and relate to their experience. For instance, how do you connect with the struggles of a parent with young kids when you've never had kids of your own? Remember, *hard* doesn't mean *impossible*. With a little practice, participation, and imagination, you can likely pull out a few similar experiences to help you relate.

Will this work be uncomfortable at times? Absolutely. Sometimes you may be unsure which questions to ask, while other times you may only be going through the motions of empathetic listening without realizing it. That's all part of the learning process. Be patient, practice introspection, and apply your what you've learned to your next interaction.

THE PLATINUM RULE

Everyone has heard of the Golden Rule: Treat others as you would want to be treated yourself. The rule might sound pretty good on paper, but, in practice, the Golden Rule asks you to assume a lot. In essence, every time you apply the Golden Rule, you're saying "I assume you should be treated in accordance with my worldview and how I was raised. I will treat you based on my own experiences rather than your own."

Isn't that a little presumptuous?

Instead of the Golden Rule, we're big believers in the Platinum Rule: *Treat others as they would want to be treated.* When you show empathy for their own perspective and experiences, you will be better able to help them.

As with most empathetic practices, the Platinum Rule requires some more work than the Golden Rule. After all, it's practically impossible to treat someone how they'd like to be treated without first getting to know them.

Further, the Platinum Rule can't easily be scaled. It requires approaching people on an individual level to try and see the world through their own unique lens. We consider that a feature, not a bug. Sometimes, moving organizational goals forward means getting buy-in from a person with whom you rarely agree. In such a situation, the Platinum Rule will get you much farther toward your own desired outcomes.

Get Walkin'

Now that you understand the value of empathy and what empathetic leadership looks like, you may be wondering: What happened to Sunil and the rest of the Bengaluru HR team?

To understand how we arrived at our solution, we need to back-track a bit—back to the early days of our culture of love. Before our pivot, Mohammad practiced what we call management by bossing around. Instead of getting out and interacting with his teams, he mostly sat in his office and told people what to do. When the going got tough, he would set increasingly unrealistic goals: five contracts a day, ten proposals, a full-fledged project plan in two days.

Are you seeing the parallel between Mohammad's misbehaviors and those of Sunil's managers? Because Mohammad didn't have a strong concept of what his teams' day-to-day reality was, and because he made no effort to find out, he had no idea how unrealistic his expectations were. So, rather than show empathy when people inevitably struggled, Mohammad showed annoyance.

Later, as Mohammad began to learn the value of empathy, he realized he didn't really understand how the company and his team members operated. He decided to change that by performing each job in the company himself. First, he served as a project manager, then as a salesperson, then as a technologist, and then—for a brief and exasperating five minutes—as a creative.

In each of these roles, Mohammad encountered unrealistic goals, which led to unintended pressure, which led to inevitable consequences and endless stress. He didn't like these experiences one bit, and he had no one to blame but himself. After all, *he* was the one who had created all these rules and processes that were now making him so miserable.

Talk about an eye-opener. In a flash of empathy, Mohammad realized the pressure he had put his team under and the impossible tasks he had asked of them. Despite his intentions, his systems and processes had only *inhibited* his teams' ability to perform.

From that day on, Mohammad vowed to test a new process, procedure, or policy before rolling it out. He needed to experiment to ensure that he wasn't asking anyone to do anything that he couldn't do. Then he needed to ask others to do the same and offer their feedback. With this realization, Mohammad had taken a huge step into the world of empathetic leadership.

Flash forward a few months later. Mohammad is in the Bengaluru office with Chris. He has just heard of the massive issue confronting HR and their recruiting processes, and he knows exactly what to do: Let the hiring managers walk a mile in Sunil's shoes.

For the next several weeks, Mohammad and Chris set out to retrain all the hiring managers in Bengaluru's HR department. Through a series of exercises, the managers were placed in the exact same situation as Sunil and his teammates—same job, same circumstances, same objectives, same timeline. Mohammad and Chris watched as, one by one, the hiring managers each came to the same realization as Sunil: There was simply no way to get all this work done and still reach their goals.

These managers had given their team members an impossible job. Once they understood this, they all responded in the same way: They walked right up to their direct reports and immediately apologized.

At that moment, they were no longer managers. They were empathetic leaders.

Less Friction, Better Results

Inside of every team, every division, and every organization, people are different from one another. That's a good thing. An organization filled with people of different backgrounds, ethnicities, and skill sets becomes greater than any one individual. However, the same differences that ultimately lead to strength and innovation can also cause friction between people if we are not careful. That's where empathy comes in.

Empathy naturally creates connections, builds cultural competence, and teaches us how to negotiate differences and connect with others through shared experiences and values. As a result, we develop our ability to uphold another pillar of love: inclusion.

That said, practicing empathy is not a free ride.

To realize the benefits of empathy, leaders must do the work of relating to every team member without excluding anyone. If you can do that, you will create an environment where people genuinely care for one another and feel empowered—both key ingredients for dynamic, high-performing teams and lower attrition.

Teams must also practice empathy between themselves consistently to see results. When they do, they build better relationships not only with each other but also with customers and clients. These improved relationships in turn lead to better-developed products and services, happier and more customers, and new—often unexpected—revenue opportunities.

Empathy—like the pillars vulnerability and trust discussed in the next two chapters—works in a positively reinforcing cycle. The greatest byproduct of empathy is more empathy. However, just like with vulnerability and trust, building empathy into your culture of love requires a leap of faith. As a leader, you must be willing to go first.

Questions for "Empathy"

- After reading this chapter, how would you describe/define empathy at work?
- Share a story about an apathetic experience where you (or someone else) took care of the business but disregarded the other person.
- How does apathetic leadership impact the culture of an organization?
- What is the main difference between sympathetic management and empathetic leadership?
- When was the last time someone jumped in the hole with you at work? When was the last time you did with someone?
- Empathy enables accountability. Share a story about someone showcasing empathetic leadership toward you. How did that make you feel?
- How do you utilize emotional intelligence to practice empathetic leadership?
- Why is the Platinum Rule better than the Golden Rule?

- How has applying the Platinum Rule impacted your leadership style?
- What value does being empathetic toward the needs of others bring you?
- When was the last time you truly practiced empathy with your team members?
- Thinking practically, what can you start doing immediately to incorporate more empathy into the way you lead?
- After reading this chapter, are you skeptical about utilizing empathy in the workplace? If so, share those thoughts with the group.
- What were some of your biggest takeaways or *ah-ha* moments from this chapter?
- Share a moment of self-awareness about your leadership after reading this chapter.
- What, if anything, will you change or adjust about how you lead or behave based on what you've read? If so, share an example.

CHAPTER 6

Vulnerability

Things weren't going well in the project management department. Every day, Jeff was astounded that an *entire team* could display so much dysfunction, ineptitude, and unaccountability. Jeff couldn't even get his head around the problem, let alone understand how to fix it.

Unsure what else to do, he struck a "cool boss" pose and implemented an open-door policy. He believed in the autonomy of his team, but he also wanted to help them solve their problems. This way, all they had to do was pop into his office and ask for help. No problem was too small. No question too dumb. He was there if they needed him.

Apparently, no one ever needed him. Not a single project manager ever came through his door. Guess he wasn't *that* cool after all.

This irritated Jeff to no end. He *knew* his team was having problems. They were struggling at every turn, making mistakes that were so baffling that it made his head spin. And yet no one sought his assistance. Why couldn't they just get out of their own ways and come seek his boundless wisdom?

One day it hit him: His project managers weren't seeking help because they weren't the problem. *He* was.

An open-door policy isn't about the door but about the person. Jeff's door might have been open, but Jeff wasn't. He dismissed or resisted his project managers' problems, preferring to give advice from on high and let them sort the details out. Jeff's door may have been open, but Jeff himself was unapproachable, intimidating, and distant, happy to disassociate from his team's problems so he wouldn't have to deal with them.

Jeff was an apathetic manager rather than as an empathetic leader.

Now that he understood the problem, next he needed to understand just how bad it was. He began asking around, both inside and outside the department, for honest feedback about his performance as a leader. It was bad—worse than he'd thought. Jeff's project managers would regularly vent to each other behind Jeff's back. They'd even go over Jeff's head to complain to Mohammad about the problems in their department. They were fed up with Jeff and his open-door policy, and he was on the verge of losing a lot of good people.

Ouch. Talk about a lot to process.

But, while this feedback hurt, Jeff was ready to change. To do that, he knew he had to do something that made him deeply uncomfortable: He had to get vulnerable with his team.

Permission to Be Human

Vulnerability, the third of our Six Pillars of Love, isn't always easy to practice. It takes a lot of courage; we repeat: a *lot*. But it's also the secret sauce of building strong human relationships; when you see someone being vulnerable, you want to be vulnerable too.

If he was going to reestablish trust with his team, Jeff knew he was going to have to get more vulnerable than he'd ever been in his professional life. First, he scheduled a series of one-on-ones with every single project manager. Each meeting began the same: with an apology. "First of all, I'd like to apologize for the type of leader I've been," Jeff said. "I'm just now realizing the harm it has caused, and I would like to take some time to explain how I view that failure." From there, Jeff would describe the specific harm his behaviors caused to that particular person. Afterward, he shared where he was in his journey as a leader, the revelation he had recently experienced, and what he intended to do about it.

By opening up, Jeff made an explicit commitment to build trust with member of his team, and he invited them to do the same. To do that, he shifted the focus of his one-on-ones from talking about work and deliverables to building relationships. The more these relationships grew, the more their empathy grew for each other. Jeff's project managers stopped trash talking him behind his back, and Jeff stopped reflexively blaming every mishap on his project managers.

Along the way, a funny thing happened: Project management grew into a high-performing team, and Jeff grew into a high-performing leader—a high-performing leader who understood and cared about his team members.

This was a hard-earned victory. After all, it takes a lot of mental energy to hold onto unforgiveness, to get caught up in office politics, to tiptoe around your manager so you can deliver bad news gently. It takes far less energy to simply share how you're feeling and move on. By sharing his concerns and his failings openly, Jeff regained the trust and empathy of his team—and in so doing, he freed up their mental energy to focus on their work rather than on office drama. Sure, they still had some problems to solve, but now that they had each other's backs, everyone was ready to dig in and solve them.

> A culture rooted in vulnerability allows people to be open and honest and share meaningful emotions. They are willing to own and learn from mistakes rather than needing to be seen as perfect.

A Wolf in Vulnerability Clothing

Vulnerability is often seen as a weakness in the workplace. We're taught to wall off our personal selves—the people we are at home—and to show up only as our professional selves. That's too bad. When we are willing to be imperfect, we can move on from our struggles and issues much faster.

But where does this resistance to vulnerability come from? Sometimes it's because an old wound hasn't healed. We've all been burned for practicing vulnerability at one point or another, and that feeling can be tough to let go of. Other times it's because we've seen someone assume the guise of vulnerability

(continued)

either to seek pity or to make someone else feel guilty. Rather than sharing out of a sense of empathy and authenticity, this person was merely manipulating the situation to their own end.

This behavior is not true vulnerability. In fact, such behavior is the antithesis of vulnerability. Sharing for the sake of manipulation is known as *floodlighting*—or deliberately obscuring the facts of a situation to confuse others and get what you want—and it's toxic to a culture of love.

Everyday Vulnerability

Vulnerability in the workplace isn't all about admitting to your mistakes and describing your deepest, darkest secrets. Sometimes vulnerability is as simple as saying "I'm sorry, I'm not in a good headspace right now. Can you handle this so I can take some time to decompress?"

Mohammad in particular has become well-known for this kind of pragmatic, everyday vulnerability. One day, for instance, Mohammad arrived at a meeting out of sorts. Earlier that day, someone had broken his trust in a way that not only injured his sense of honor but that raised important legal questions.

It was a lot to process, and Mohammad found himself distracted and angry in that meeting. But while old Mohammad would have tried to power through the meeting with a chip on his shoulder (or worse), new Mohammad had the self-awareness to come clean with the rest of the team. He shared his problem and asked for a little space to clear his head, and the rest of us were more than happy to oblige.

In our eyes, it wasn't just a matter of giving Mohammad space. As part of Mohammad's support structure, we knew that the problem was weighing on him and that he was asking for help. After seeing that Mohammad had cleared the rest of his calendar for the day, we made sure to check in on him to offer support and see if there was anything else we could do.

Many CEOs wouldn't have felt like they could show their emotions like that, much less walk away from their work for a day. However, by practicing vulnerability in this way, Mohammad took care of both himself and his team, which no longer was at risk of dealing with any potential misbehaviors. Better still, this show of vulnerability reinforced the trust and empathy he had placed in his team, invited them to understand him more deeply, and showcased the right behaviors for them to emulate.

We often resist sharing our struggles with others, and yet we usually feel better when we do. When you close yourself off to support, you'll never realize it was available. After all, it's hard for others to be empathetic toward your situation if you don't share your situation in the first place. However, by creating an environment for others to have empathy toward you, you also create a support system of people ready to help however possible.

That's what vulnerability is all about. Sharing your struggles may not change the situation, but it *does* contribute to feelings of safety, understanding, and resilience. When Mohammad arrived at his next set of meetings the next day, he was engaged, warm, and grateful for the opportunity to clear his head.

It's Okay to Be Uncertain

At his previous job, Chris witnessed a moment of vulnerability that completely altered his relationship to problem-solving. At the time he was working for a woman who presented a tough, unimpeachable front 99 percent of the time. One day, however, as they were working through a tough challenge, she let her guard down. "If I'm being honest," she said, "I have no idea how to figure this situation out."

In that moment, his coworker's mask slipped, and Chris could see who she really was. Suddenly Chris understood that no one had all the answers—not even the people he deeply admired. From that moment onward, he approached every problem with a new mindset. It wasn't about having all the answers but about figuring those answers out! By sharing with others and being transparent about his process, he could get there, no matter how messy and uncertain the road was ahead.

A Practice of Renewal

Vulnerability doesn't happen by accident. You don't wake up one day, flip a switch, and suddenly become vulnerable. Showing vulnerability requires attention, authenticity, humility, and active engagement with others.

It took a great deal of humility for Jeff to seek out feedback, endure harsh truths, and then admit his shortcomings to his team. But without that effort, he wouldn't have ever attempted to solve the problem. Today Jeff makes active feedback a regular part of his development as he works to become a better leader. The practice is contagious. When project managers see Jeff on a mission to improve, they can't help but want to do the same. When they see Jeff owning up to a mistake, they understand they have permission to make their own mistakes as well.

To create that kind of space within your team, here are a few bits of advice.

First, let go of ego. It's easy to get caught up in this idea that we must be invincible, that we can't show weakness by admitting we've ever failed. But such a mindset causes much more harm than good.

A successful organization is nothing but a series of mistakes that turned into opportunities. Your job isn't to be perfect all the time. It's to share what's on your mind so that others can bring their ideas to the table and contribute to your mutual success. Viewed from that lens, vulnerability is a sign of strength. Shy away from that strength, and you risk missing out on the very opportunities that could propel your organization forward.

Second, don't be mean. Vulnerability is not an excuse to hurt others or threaten their psychological safety but a chance to understand each other and grow from the experience. Be your true, authentic self, but also be your *best* self. There's no need to be blunt, rude, or destructive to others.

Applied correctly, vulnerability promotes psychological safety. We work better when we know we have permission to be uncertain, to make mistakes, and to take ownership of those mistakes without ridicule or blame. Teams operating in a psychologically safe environment communicate better, solve problems more effectively, and are more creative and innovative.

That makes sense. If you know you can mess up and be heard fairly, you don't have to waste time on unnecessary bureaucracy. You avoid wasted days and weeks of worry. You understand you have opportunities to address mistakes and move on. Most important, you have permission to take risks, try something new, and embrace the results whether things work out perfectly or not.

This is precisely what happened to Jeff and his project management team. It took time for Jeff to build new working relationships with his project managers, to understand their struggles and respond with empathy, and to better understand the nuances of the project manager role and how he could better facilitate it.

Jeff wouldn't have accomplished any of this if his team suspected he wasn't committed to them. They had to hear him say he'd never dealt with clients on the level that they had and that he had never managed projects the way they had. They had to see him go to client meetings and learn to manage a project from the ground up. They had to see him admit what he didn't know and respond with empathy to them. They had to see him earn that credibility by showing up every day.

These days the project management team is one of the strongest at Softway. Mohammad calls them his "mini-CEOs" and regularly recruits from that team for senior leadership roles. (See Chapter 14.) He credits the newfound strength of the project management team to Jeff—specifically, to Jeff's willingness to be vulnerable and commit to change.

Jeff isn't ready to take all the credit for this transformation. However, he has seen the difference in the close relationships he has built with his project managers. Jeff's cool-boss, open-door policy days may be over, but now his team knows—they *trust*—that he is always there to listen and lend a hand.

Leadership in a culture of love is being vulnerable in the face of struggle and taking ownership for your part in that struggle. It's saying you don't know everything, but you want to work with the team. You're committed to working with them.

This concept is simple, but it takes tremendous courage. After all, it's not easy to let your guard down. It's not easy to admit that you aren't perfect. It's not easy to take off the armor you've put on as a result of previous experiences, relationships, and workplaces—and to stop pretending to be invincible. But the more you do it, the more you give permission to others to do it as well.

Questions for "Vulnerability"

♦ Why is vulnerability the secret sauce of human connection?

♦ Thinking practically, what does vulnerability in the workplace look like for you?

♦ Why is vulnerability in the workplace so hard?

♦ What have you experienced when leaders demonstrate vulnerability?

♦ In the past, what's held you back from openly admitting to mistakes?

♦ How can vulnerability become toxic, and what can you do to prevent such toxicity?

♦ How do you know that your vulnerability has an impact on your coworkers?

♦ When is it difficult for you to practice vulnerability?

♦ Share a story about a moment when you practiced everyday vulnerability.

♦ Share about a moment when you had to practice vulnerability with the group. What did it take to get to that place? How did it feel?

♦ Share a recent failure with the group. What did you learn from it?

♦ Thinking practically, what can you start doing immediately to incorporate more vulnerability into the way you lead?

♦ After reading this chapter, are you skeptical about utilizing vulnerability in the workplace? If so, share those thoughts with the group.

♦ What were some of your biggest takeaways or *ah-ha* moments from this chapter?

♦ Share a moment of self-awareness about your leadership after reading this chapter.

♦ What, if anything, will you change or adjust about how you lead or behave based on what you've read?

CHAPTER 7

Trust

Frank does not have a four-year degree. There, we said it.

He could have one, but instead he chose to join his dad's startup after earning his associate's degree. Joining his dad's technology company turned out to be one of the best decisions he ever made. First, joining a startup at such a young age taught Frank some real-world lessons that a college can't. Second, after his father's sudden passing at fifty, when Frank was just twenty-six, those precious few years became invaluable.

Frank also came to learn about Softway through his dad's company, since his dad was an early client. Through his work with Softway and other organizations, Frank saw another business opportunity—so, in true entrepreneurial fashion, he co-created another company. Then, just four months after incorporating his new company, he sold it to Softway and joined our leadership team.

All this good fortune likely wouldn't have happened if Frank had chosen to follow a traditional path, and he is proud of everything he has accomplished. But even to this day, he is sensitive about the fact that he doesn't have a four-year or more advanced degree.

Yep, Frank exhibits all the classic signs of impostor syndrome. As part of an organization where many of his coworkers have two, three, or more degrees, he sometimes feels like the odd person out. Frank knows that he's been successful, but he fears that one day his peers will turn on him. They won't invite him to meetings, they'll shun him around the espresso machine and otherwise treat him as a bona fide impostor.

To compensate for this fear, Frank adopted some unique behaviors. Sometimes he would just shut down. If he heard his teammates speaking negatively about people without college degrees, Frank would fall silent, look down at the floor, and then walk away. Other times, especially when meeting with high-profile clients, Frank would prepare to lie about his degree and where he earned it, just in case. He would even research professors at the school in case he needed to elaborate on his experience. Fortunately, he never had to play that card.

This behavior may sound extreme, but from Frank's point of view, he was protecting Softway. Many of the company's clients and decision makers had multiple advanced degrees. Some even had doctorates. Frank was certain that if he were found out, no one would want to do business with him or the company.

Frank eventually realized his fear and misbehaviors were untenable. So one day, in the spirit of bringing his full self to work, he decided to tell the truth, even if he didn't know how it would turn out. Rather than fear what he couldn't control, Frank chose to trust his teammates to lift him up.

One of the first people Frank confided in was Jeff. By this time, Frank and Jeff had been collaborating for years—ranging from high-end consulting with Softway's most prestigious clients, to short-form comedy sketches seen only on Snapchat. Jeff had become not only a coworker but also Frank's friend. However, because Jeff did have a bachelor's degree, Frank was terrified Jeff might judge him.

One day Frank took a leap of faith and came clean.

"That's it?" Jeff shrugged. "I don't care about any of that, man. You're still Frank. You're still the person I know and love and care about."

This was exactly the kind of validation Frank was hoping for—especially from someone like Jeff, whom he trusted and admired. He needed to know that his teammates accepted him for who he was, not for the degrees he did or didn't hold.

As Frank came clean to more and more teammates, most of their responses matched Jeff's. He felt like he was revealing some big secret, but their understated reactions said otherwise. His work and work ethic already spoke volumes. His teammates knew this and accepted him for who he was.

Frank's impostor syndrome didn't disappear completely as a result of these conversations, but it did shrink quite a bit. Any of Frank's teammates could have used this knowledge against him. Instead, they responded with empathy, thanked him for sharing, and reaffirmed their personal and professional bonds with him.

Stories like this highlight why trust is one of our Six Pillars of Love. When we trust our teammates, we have confidence in their integrity, strength, and ability to perform a difficult task, manage a responsibility, and maintain psychological safety. It's not easy to open up to someone and share a part of yourself that could be used against you. In a culture of love, however, that trust should always be rewarded. But to do that, we must learn to push beyond superficial forms of trust and work toward something deeper.

The Two Kinds of Trust

Usually, when we think of trust, we think of *predictive trust*. Predictive trust is based on the idea that you know someone well enough to predict what they may think or do. For instance:

- ◆ You trust that Mohammad will be eager to talk about the most recent University of Houston football game.
- ◆ You trust that Chris will find a way to work a Beyoncé reference into the conversation.
- ◆ You trust that Frank will brew a perfect cup of coffee with his trusty Hario V60 before the next meeting starts.
- ◆ You trust that Jeff will break out one of his many, many board games whenever you're over for a dinner party.

Predictive trust is stable, but it's also superficial. It's based on patterns and perception, not on relationships. So, when Frank shared that he didn't have a four-year degree, a small group responded to this information with jealousy and anger.

During meetings, these teammates became uninterested in Frank's feedback because—as they stated in their own words—they believed he wasn't qualified to have an opinion. Further, they were unwilling to trust Frank with new responsibilities. If he hadn't done something before (or because he didn't have a piece of paper that said he could do it), then they didn't believe he was capable.

This is the problem with predictive trust: It limits a person only to a specific aspect of who they are and what they have done in the past. Rather than promote growth, predictive trust leads to stagnation—which is exactly what happened to Frank's team after these bad actors chose to see Frank only in terms of his education. After their misbehaviors had gone on for a while, Frank decided that he was tired of being marginalized, verbally attacked, emotionally abused, and blocked out of important decisions. So, one night during a trip to San Francisco, Frank shared his story and the fallout that ensued with Chris.

This got Chris thinking. What could he do to better include Frank at the table? It's easy to make an offhand reference to the college experience—dorm life, tailgate parties, all-nighters, and so on. These stories work because they help forge connections with others in the dominant group. (See Chapter 4.) Now that Chris knew Frank *didn't* share those experiences, he thought about all the times he had unintentionally marginalized his friend. Considering the insecurity Frank felt about his education, Chris was grateful that Frank had confided in him.

Through this exchange, Chris and Frank formed a deeper trust—what is known as *vulnerability-based trust.*

Vulnerability-based trust is built out of what the *Harvard Business Review* refers to as the three elements of trust: relationships, expertise, and consistency. Each element is important, but relationships are key. If a person is inconsistent or lacks crucial expertise, trust in that person might take a hit, but it can be rebuilt. If a person betrays a relationship, however, they may never earn trust with the other person again.[1]

Through the lens of vulnerability-based trust, Frank's lack of a four-year degree didn't matter. Mohammad knew Frank's education when he hired him, and he didn't care. Why? Because he also knew that Frank had both the expertise and the consistency to contribute to the company, think creatively, and deliver excellent service to Softway's clients. Over the next several years, Frank delivered time and time again. Mohammad, Jeff, and Chris knew they could predict that he would continue to deliver.

However, because of their relationship with Frank, their trust extended further. They didn't just trust Frank to deliver what he knew; they trusted Frank to grow *beyond* his current skill set. They empowered Frank to operate with uncertainty, risk, and emotional exposure because they knew a secret: The more you practice vulnerability-based trust with others, the more they will reward that trust through exemplary effort.

Unfortunately, certain members of Frank's team hadn't yet embraced vulnerability-based trust. So, when they saw Mohammad or others giving Frank new responsibilities, they openly revolted. "I spent a lot of money earning my degree," one team member told Mohammad, "and Frank thinks he can tell *me* what to do?!"

Mohammad heard their objections, but he also knew they were meaningless. Frank consistently exceeded expectations in his job and had earned every new responsibility he was given—and then some.

When teams operate from a place of predictive trust, they see their work only in terms of what they know rather than what is *possible*. They're reluctant to experiment, to explore, or otherwise to take risks. Worse, they're reluctant to encourage that behavior in others. They don't trust what they don't know, and therefore their trajectory is limited. They never grow. Fortunately, the spell of predictive trust can be broken. Anyone can learn to practice vulnerability-based trust. But the change has to start at the top.

Where's the Trust?

Leadership without trust isn't leadership at all—it's management. Often, we don't recognize a trust deficit until it's too late: either a team has wasted massive amounts of time and energy, or it has failed altogether.

To avoid such an outcome, leaders must be willing to both trust and be trusted. Further, they must be able to forgive and ask for forgiveness.

These are the signs of true servant leadership. (See Chapters 9 and 10.)

How to Take a Leap of Faith (and Stick the Landing)

Ask the members of a team broadly whether they trust each other, and they'll invariably say yes. However, ask a few more targeted questions, and things start to get more interesting:

- How often do you give each other feedback?
- How do you handle mistakes?
- Are you willing to talk to a coworker directly and plainly about their mistake even if it hurts their feelings? Or do you beat around the bush?

Questions like this often reveal that a team's predictive trust is only about an inch deep. They trust each other to get the job done. Nothing more, nothing less.

Vulnerability-based trust means telling people hard truths—not out of spite, but out of a desire to help someone look out for their best interests. This constructive accountability helps eliminate fear, improve loyalty, and build high-performing teams.

Now, here's the tricky part: Creating vulnerable trust in the workplace can be a bit of a catch-22. You need trust to build high-performing teams, and that trust is built on the kind of deep relationships that grow over time. The question, then, is what happens when a new person joins a team? How do you uphold the tenets of a culture of love and practice vulnerability-based trust with someone you hardly know? If only there were a way to build vulnerable trust quickly *and* effectively.

As it turns out, there is. In 1997, a team of researchers found that they could rapidly create strong interpersonal relationships between total strangers.[2] Their methodology was fairly straightforward. Starting with a randomly selected group of people, the researchers split the participants into pairs, where the participants would take turns asking each other a set of thirty-six questions. Ranging from lighthearted to poignant, these questions included:

- Given the choice of anyone in the world, whom would you want as a dinner guest?
- What's your most treasured memory?

◆ If you could change anything about the way you were raised, what would it be?

Through these questions, the participants developed a deep sense of mutual respect and affinity for each other. In fact, many of the participants remained friends long after the experiment—and two even ended up getting married. Seeing these results, the researchers concluded that vulnerability does not require a preexisting relationship to be effective. Given the right conditions, any two people can connect and develop vulnerable trust with each other.[3]

In 2018, driven by our own desire to accelerate the process of building vulnerability-based trust in our organization, we decided to adapt this experiment to a business environment, selecting the most appropriate questions for our purposes and using ourselves as guinea pigs. Even though we knew what to expect, the results were still shocking. Before, we would look around our team and see each other largely in terms of the reports that they owed us, their successes and failures at work, or their educational attainment. After, we saw each other as complex, fascinating human beings—people with parents, siblings, partners, and children; people with aspirations and insecurities; people who were just trying to find their way in the world like everyone else.

This experiment changed both how we saw each other and how we worked together. If Jeff was working alongside Frank, for instance, and he saw that Frank was having trouble getting something done, Jeff had trust and compassion for Frank's situation. Rather than assume he was lazy, making excuses, or incompetent because he lacked a degree, Jeff saw Frank as a human being who had a problem he was trying to solve.

Encouraged by these results, we then adapted this exercise for our Culture Rise leadership workshops to see if we could rapidly create growth and connection among our participants. Once again, the results were breathtaking. Leaders were able to be vulnerable and answer questions that people generally say you shouldn't do at work. Hardened industry vets cried and hugged. People who had worked together side-by-side for a decade or more now saw each other in a completely new light. Participants walked away with a concentrated dose of trust, transformed in their ability to work within their teams and drive results in their organization.

The Sure Signs of Trust

How do you know when your teams are practicing vulnerability-based trust? Here are a few sure signs that you have built high-performing teams where each person cares for each other:

- Team members know that their deficiencies won't be used against them.
- Team members are quick to resolve disputes and conflicts and don't stoop to gossip or slander.
- Team members act without concern for protecting themselves.
- Team members have more than a surface-level knowledge of those they work with.

In July 2019, several months after we first deployed this exercise during a Culture Rise event, the University of Sydney released research that validated our approach as more effective than traditional trust-building exercises.[4] Through the thirty-six questions experiment, we've learned how to take a leap of faith and stick the landing. It's not easy to be vulnerable with someone—whether you've just met or whether you've known that person for years. But if you can, the payoff in trust is almost immediate. When someone sees the faith you've put in them, they will seek to both live up to that trust and place the same trust in you.

Trust in Your Full Self

Frank still struggles with impostor syndrome during client meetings. No matter how many times he has proven himself, no matter how much he has accomplished, he still goes in feeling as if he has something more to prove.

That's the thing with impostor syndrome; it never really goes away. However, you have a choice over how you respond to it: Ignore it and let it fester, or acknowledge it and move on. That's precisely why Frank chose to tell this story here, in the fourth of our Six Pillars of Love. After all, what better way to confront those pesky impostor feelings than to tell the world one of your deepest insecurities? In that way, the story in this chapter is just Frank doubling down on a choice he made long ago: to trust his teammates with the knowledge of his full self and whatever perceived flaws that might entail.

Yes, sometimes people will punish you for this kind of vulnerability, as they did with Frank. But in those moments, shutting won't get you anywhere. The more we turn away from trust and vulnerability, the more we feel out of step with those around us, and the more alone we grow. Vulnerability is often scary in the moment, but the long-term benefits far outweigh any short-term pains. These days Frank knows that when you trust your team to have your back, any supposed shortcomings no longer define you. They just become part of your full self.

Get Vulnerable. Get Trustin'

Find our free vulnerability toolkit and more trust-based resources at LoveAsAStrategy.com/resources.

Questions for "Trust"

- If you've ever struggled with imposter syndrome like Frank, how has it shown up in your behavior with your coworkers?
- How has imposter syndrome hindered or helped you at work?
- What are some ways you can support those who struggle with imposter syndrome?
- How do you showcase trust to your team?
- With whom do you practice predictive trust?
- Why do you think we often default to predictive trust?
- Share a few examples of how you've demonstrated predictive trust to others at your workplace.
- Why is relationship the determining factor in developing vulnerability-based trust?
- Share a few examples of how you've demonstrated vulnerability-based trust to others at your workplace.

- What's holding you back from building deeper connections with your colleagues?
- How do you know when your team members are truly practicing vulnerability-based trust?
- If you've ever taken the leap and shared your full-self with colleagues, what happened as a result?
- Thinking practically, what can you start doing immediately to incorporate more trust into the way you lead?
- After reading this chapter, are you skeptical about utilizing vulnerability-based trust in the workplace? If so, share those thoughts with the group.
- What were some of your biggest takeaways or *ah-ha* moments from this chapter?
- Share a moment of self-awareness about your leadership after reading this chapter.
- What, if anything, will you change or adjust about how you lead or behave based on what you've read?

Notes

1. Jack Zenger and Joseph Folkman, "The 3 Elements of Trust," *Harvard Business Review*, February 5, 2019. https://hbr.org/2019/02/the-3-elements-of-trust

2. Arthur Aron, Edward Melinat, Elaine N. Aron, Robert D. Vallone, and Renee J. Bator, "The Experimental Generation of Interpersonal Closeness: A Procedure and Some Preliminary Findings," *Personality and Social Psychology Bulletin* 23, no. 4 (April 1997): 363–377. https://doi.org/10.1177%2F0146167297234003

3. Daniel Jones, "The 36 Questions That Lead to Love," *New York Times*, January 9, 2015. https://www.nytimes.com/2015/01/09/style/no-37-big-wedding-or-small.html

4. Julien Pollack and Petr Matous, University of Sydney, "It Could Pay to Get Personal at Work—Here's Why," July 17, 2019. https://www.sydney.edu.au/news-opinion/news/2019/07/17/It-could-pay-to-get-personal-at-work-heres-why.html

CHAPTER 8

Empowerment

Frank was feeling really, really good about himself.

He had every reason to. It was February 2020, and Frank had taken the "new year, new me" maxim literally. He'd lost about eighty-five pounds (and two chins) over the past six months (no joke) and looked like a totally different person.

Right around that same time, Softway was preparing a big marketing blitz for new opportunities and initiatives. As part of that effort, the team had scheduled a two-day photo shoot. Thrilled at the idea of updating his company headshot, Frank figured he could pop in, snap a few photos, and then pop back out. Easy-peasy.

All that was left to do was to let Maggie know his plans.

"Nope," Maggie said flatly when he brought up his big idea.

Well, *that* wasn't the answer Frank expected to hear. "Uh, why?"

"That's not what this shoot is for," she said. "We'll have to do headshots another time."

"But. . .but my face has changed," Frank said sheepishly. "I don't look like my old picture anymore. It will only take a minute."

Maggie nodded. "You look great. Really. But if I let you get a new headshot, it opens the floodgates and pushes back our deliverables. I can't do it."

"I understand. That's totally fine," Frank said.

But it wasn't fine. Frank could see why Maggie, a relatively new hire at the time, insisted on setting boundaries, but *come on*. How much could a headshot possibly set deliverables back?

The next day, in the mood for a little misbehavin', Frank walked up to a different project manager. "Hey, uh, could you ask Maggie if we have time to sneak in a headshot during that photo shoot?"

A few minutes later, the project manager came back. "Maggie said, and I quote, 'Please tell Frank that this photoshoot is not for headshots.' Sorry, Frank."

Dang. Maggie was good.

But Frank was undeterred. *We'll just see what happens next week,* Frank told himself.

Soon the day of the photoshoot arrived. Everything was going off without a hitch. People were laughing and having a great time as we captured shot after marvelous shot. When lunch rolled around, the photographer walked over to Frank, who had been patiently (but quite conspicuously) waiting around.

"Hey, Frank," he said, "I've got a few minutes before I head off to lunch. I hear you were hoping to get a new headshot." *Victory!*

Frank stood up to accept. . .and then sat right back down. Suddenly he felt gross.

"No thanks, man."

"Are you sure? It's really no trouble," the photographer said.

"I know, but today is not about headshots," Frank said. "It's about marketing deliverables."

The photographer shrugged and headed off for lunch.

Empowerment Isn't Just a Word

So, what happened there? Why did Frank end up having second thoughts? At the very last moment, Frank realized that getting that headshot wasn't his call to make. It was Maggie's. The headshot wasn't that big of a deal, but going behind Maggie's back to get it *was.*

Through countless small moments like these, we have learned that empowerment isn't just a word but an action. If Maggie was empowered to run the photoshoot, then Frank's job was to step aside and let her do her job—to make decisions, own her tasks and responsibilities, and perform that work as she saw fit. As long as she performed her job within the scope and context of the desired business outcomes, she was free to decide the best path to get there.

When you are empowered to do your job, you feel valued, trusted, respected, and included. You feel as if you can bring your full self to work, contribute to a culture of love, and help grow the organization.

On the day of the photoshoot, Maggie had decided to cut out all distractions and focus only on our target marketing outcomes. Once Frank remembered that this was her decision to make, he saw his own behavior in a different light. Maggie was right to tell Frank no, and he was wrong for trying to manipulate the situation to get his way. Had Frank followed through with his plan, he would have disempowered Maggie, broken her trust, and hampered her ability to perform from that point forward. It would have encouraged the notion that Softway's leaders don't believe in a culture of love when they don't get their way.

Luckily, at the last minute, Frank's good nature won out, he owned up to his misbehaviors, and he apologized to Maggie the next day.

A few weeks later, working through the appropriate channels, Frank finally got his new headshot. (And he looked *good*.)

Clear the Path

In a culture of love, empowering a team member isn't about putting someone in charge and then ignoring them. It's about setting them up for success. When choosing to empower someone, ask yourself:

- ◆ Have I given this person everything they need and explained the outcomes and goals I expect?
- ◆ Have I given them coaching?
- ◆ Am I spending time to mentor and nurture this person in their role?
- ◆ Have I given this person the information, tools, and access they need to be successful?
- ◆ Am I removing blocks and obstacles?

(continued)

♦ Do I respect their decisions, even when those decisions inconvenience me?

You can remain engaged and available without intervening or micromanaging the process. Instead of handing your team members answers, clear their path so they can arrive at the answers themselves. Sometimes it can be difficult to avoid the impulse to intervene, but we've seen firsthand that when you give someone a chance, they usually rise to the occasion.

The Power of Empowerment

If Frank and Maggie's story was Empowerment 101, this next story is Empowerment 202: executing in a high-stakes situation.

Our Culture Rise training event began with an impossible task. One day the leadership experience didn't exist at all. The next day it was a multimillion-dollar business opportunity that gave rise to an entirely new subsidiary of Softway (Culture+) and a smattering of offerings for organizations of all sizes. *Talk about empowerment.* And it happened completely out of the blue. One day one of our main clients asked us if we could help them transform into a culture of love. They had been so impressed by our own transformation journey that they wanted us to teach them our secret sauce, and they were willing to pay top dollar for the privilege.

We were thrilled at the opportunity, but there was just one problem: We'd never considered making our teachings a product or client experience. Now, all of a sudden, we only had two weeks to convert our internal programs into a public-facing workshop. How do you design two days' worth of love-based content for twenty-five business leaders? Where could we find a good venue and caterers on such short notice? What did we need to include in the experience that would justify a multimillion-dollar investment?

Full of questions but short on answers, Mohammad dove into the challenge headfirst—and quickly found that he was in way over his head. The more he got done, the more he realized how much he had to do (and that he didn't know how to do it). So, Mohammad swallowed his pride and asked a power trio of project managers for their help.

As it turned out, our power trio of Erin, Ashley, and Chelsie had the perfect combination of experience to help our efforts soar. Chelsie had an extensive background in event planning, and Erin and Ashley had broad knowledge and logistical experience from working in the service industry. Before we knew it, we had a venue, a caterer, and a working document of how we would run the show (which we still use to this day).

Here is where trust and vulnerability intersect with empowerment. We had never seen any of our project managers manage a project like this. But we did know who they were and what they were capable of. So, embracing vulnerability-based trust, we looked them right in the eye, admitted that we had no idea what we were doing, and asked for help.

For the next two weeks, Erin, Ashley, and Chelsie did everything in their power to make the event a success. No detail was too small. Music cues? Check. Ambient lighting? Check. Greenery and other small decorative touches? Check. Had we continued to try to manage the process ourselves, all these crucial details would have been missed.

Soon the big day was upon us, and we were ready to execute. Did everything go off without a hitch? Of course not. Mistakes were made—and we were better off for it.

The biggest mistake was that we hadn't ordered nearly enough food. As the food began to run out, we watched in horror as attendees began to grumble and get antsy. Luckily, Ashley was on it. The moment she realized the situation, she got Frank's attention, and together they alerted Mohammad. "These people are struggling," Frank said. "If we don't feed them soon, they're going to leave and go find more food themselves. I don't care if we order pizza—we need to do something."

"Okay," Mohammad said. "Let's get pizza!"

Ashley put in the order, hopped in her car, and returned with twenty boxes of fresh, delicious pizza just thirty minutes later.

Leaders can try as much as they want to prevent their teams from making mistakes. But in doing so, they lose sight of the opportunities for growth that mistakes provide us with. Even worse, they deny their team members opportunities to take on new challenges, push the organization in unexpected directions, or, in this case, work creatively in the moment to find solutions to pressing problems.

We made a mistake not ordering enough food for the workshop. But we also rolled with the punches and took full ownership of the situation. While Ashley was out getting pizza, Mohammad spoke to our attendees. He apologized for the error, explained that we'd never run this program before, and then explained what we were doing to make it right.

The attendees were blown away. In fact, as a few of them explained afterward, our little mishap gave them a chance to see our teachings play out in real time. During a tense situation, we showed them how we loved, cared for, empowered, and trusted each other. This unscripted display not only humanized us but also made a more compelling case for a culture of love than all our carefully crafted content. At that moment, our attendees saw that we weren't merely consultants looking to win a bid but practitioners on a mission to change hearts and minds.

Not long after, our client awarded us the contract. Today, the Culture Rise leadership event has helped us teach Love as a Business Strategy to thousands of leaders around the world.

Practice in the Small Moments

Empowerment isn't easy. It goes against some of our strongest impulses. That's why it's so important to practice in low-stakes moments, as when Frank almost maneuvered around Maggie to get a new headshot. If you can honor your commitment to empowerment when nothing's on the line, you can do it in the big, high-stakes moments too.

In the two weeks leading up to our Culture Rise pilot, our commitment to empowerment was frequently put to the test. Mohammad in particular found it difficult to relinquish control and often stepped in and tried to be more hands-on in the planning process.

Every time he did, our power trio of project managers always said the same thing: "Mohammad, relax. We've got this. Please *leave us alone* so we can do what we need to do."

Eventually he got the message, and he stepped out of their way for good. It was at that moment that our team began firing on all cylinders. No sugarcoating it: Those two weeks were a grind. But for those of us who went through it, it was also one of our favorite experiences working at Softway.

When you empower someone from a place of vulnerability, when that person sees that you trust and believe in them, it unlocks what we call the power of empowerment. From that point on, the person will go out of their way to succeed—not out of fear, but because they want to reward the trust they were given. This is the feeling that made all those long nights worth it—and what made the Culture Rise pilot such a resounding success, mistakes and all.

Bringing Culture Rise to You

Since 2018, the Culture Rise leadership experience has helped thousands of leaders bring a culture of love to their organizations. And we've gotten a lot better at it since that first pilot.

If you are interested in learning more about our culture and change offerings and experiences, or hosting a Culture Rise for your organization, please visit www.Culture-plus.com.

Questions for "Empowerment"

- From the story of Frank's headshot, what do you think the difference is between delegation and empowerment?
- Share a story about when you've truly felt the power of empowerment. How did that change the work you did?
- In what situations would it be challenging for you to empower others? Why?
- Thinking introspectively—do you have a hard time empowering others? Why do you think that is?
- Whom can you start to empower more in your team?
- How does it feel to truly empower others? Share a story of success and failure.
- Why is it so hard for leaders to empower others? What do you think is the root cause of this struggle?
- What does it look like when people in your organization are not empowered?
- How does empowerment unlock the other pillars of love?
- Share a story about how you've empowered others in the small moments.

- Thinking practically, what can you start doing immediately to incorporate more empowerment into the way you lead?
- After reading this chapter, are you skeptical about the idea of empowering others in the workplace? If so, share those thoughts with the group.
- What were some of your biggest takeaways or *ah-ha* moments from this chapter?
- Share a moment of self-awareness about your leadership after reading this chapter.
- What, if anything, will you change or adjust about how you lead or behave based on what you've read?

CHAPTER 9

Forgiveness

It was 2017. Softway was two years into its embrace of Love as a Business Strategy. The effort had required both personal and organizational sacrifice, but Mohammad was proud of what he and his company had accomplished. As far as he could tell, it was working. Softway had a culture of love. It was fragile, but it was there.

Eager to celebrate all they had accomplished as a company, Mohammad traveled to India to hold an all-hands meeting with his team. To open the meeting, he asked what he thought would be a simple question: "How many of you believe that trust has improved between you and me?"

Two people raised their hands.

Out of a hundred.

Mohammad felt absolutely gutted. How could it be true, after all this time, that still no one trusted him? Were all those policy changes useless? Had all the work he'd done to adopt and embody a culture of love meant nothing?

What a disappointment. Feeling his anger swell and not wanting to lash out and say something that would make the moment even worse, Mohammad abruptly ended the meeting and hurried out of the room.

It took Mohammad two days of hard introspection before he knew what he should do. Only then did he understand what was still missing.

Softway had done a lot of good work over the past two years. But there was one thing during that time that Mohammad hadn't done: hold himself accountable for the person he'd been *before* embracing the path of love. Mohammad may have improved his behavior since then, but his team hadn't forgotten—or forgiven—the person he once was.

It was time to say he was sorry and back it up with action.

Toward the end of his visit, Mohammad held another meeting with the same group. Standing before them, his stomach in knots, he began to speak.

"I realize that I was asking you to trust me when I didn't show you trust first." He paused a moment to gather himself. "I want to apologize for the trouble both my behavior and my policies have caused you. I am sorry to everyone, both current and former employees and their families. I know that I have caused you harm, and I want to do better."

Then Mohammad held up the two-year contract that every employee in India had signed. In the contract, his team members had agreed to pay Softway $2,500 if they quit before the two years were up.

"This contract is another sign that I have not demonstrated trust in you." He began tearing the contract in half. "From here on out, none of you are obligated to this contract. If you choose to leave, I understand, and I will not seek damages. Please forgive me."

Tears streaming down his face, Mohammad let the torn-up contract fall to the floor. Then, once again overcome by his emotions, he ended the meeting and left the hall.

The rest of the trip passed without incident. On the last night, Mohammad attended a farewell gathering, where his team presented him with a surprise: a book filled with messages for him from everyone in the company. The title of that book was *We Love You and We Trust You, Moh.*

Mohammad broke down. . .again. This time, though, he was crying tears of joy. They had heard him. They had seen his heart. Finally, they *trusted* him.

A week earlier, Mohammad's team had greeted him with skepticism and distrust. Now they had embraced him as a leader worthy of their trust, support, and love. His authenticity and humility had opened a door that had been tightly shut.

Only two people quit as a result of Mohammad's tearing up that contract. He had been afraid of a mass exodus. But he knew he couldn't expect them to trust him unless he trusted them first and truly owned up to what he had done.

> Forgiveness is the ability to look past someone's mistakes, shortcomings, or offensive actions, and continue to build a relationship.

Forgiveness Is a Verb

In Christianity, there's an axiom that God forgives, putting the bad things people have done as far from them as the east is from the west. In Western culture, this idea is often expressed as "forgive and forget."

But let's be honest. We're all human. We may forgive, but we never forget completely. When Mohammad's team in India forgave him, they all didn't experience collective amnesia from that moment onward. They still remembered who Mohammad had been, but they chose to love, trust, and pursue a productive relationship with him anyway.

This willingness to forgive is an important concept to understand in any relationship. Forgiveness is not a one-and-done event but rather an ongoing, renewing process. For instance, Mohammad may have earned his team's forgiveness in India, but that didn't mean he behaved perfectly from that point on.

In a culture of love, we practice forgiveness by looking past an individual's mistakes and continuing to build a relationship. We all unintentionally hurt each other through the course of our messy, imperfect lives. But if we can acknowledge that, then we can learn to forgive bidirectionally. Teams can forgive leaders. Leaders can forgive teams. And team members can forgive each other.

We've seen this process at play, and we know that it works. But only if everyone in the organization commits to the process.

An Apology Without Action. . .

Asking for forgiveness isn't a particularly difficult action to understand. The challenge is in allowing ourselves to be vulnerable and take the leap. Most leaders find it all but impossible to ask for forgiveness. But as Mohammad's story shows, sometimes it's essential for an organization to move forward. In a very real way, our entire future as a company hinged on Mohammad's ability to humble himself on that trip.

Equally important is accountability. Imagine that Jeff and Frank share an office. They agree to clean up after themselves and keep their work areas neat, but lately Jeff has been ignoring that responsibility. Frank brings this up to Jeff, and Jeff apologizes. "I'm so sorry I've been leaving messes lately, Frank," Jeff says. "I'll be better about it from now on."

A day goes by. Then a week. Then a month. And Jeff is still leaving messes, he shows no signs of changing, and Frank is mad. Where once Jeff had an opportunity to strengthen his relationship with Frank, he has now damaged Frank's trust in him and harmed that relationship further.

While this particular lesson is hypothetical (Jeff is a pretty clean guy everywhere except the pickleball court, where he plays dirty), the dynamic it illustrates is real. In situations like this, actions really do speak louder than intentions. Forgiveness loses its potency quickly if no action follows the apology.

You cannot ask forgiveness if you do not acknowledge fault, which means you must possess the emotional intelligence and self-awareness to know when you have broken someone's trust. Without understanding how you caused this break, you cannot attempt to repair it. Then, to seek true forgiveness and rebuild that relationship, you must communicate your understanding in both speech and action.

Yes, Forgiveness Is Blind

As hard as it can be to ask for forgiveness, offering forgiveness can be even harder. It took two full years for our team in India to forgive Mohammad for the hurt he had caused before—and even then, it took a leap of faith for them to do so.

In order to forgive, we must be willing to see the goodness in the person we are forgiving. A sincere apology helps bring those qualities front and center. That said, we don't always have the benefit of a dramatic apology like Mohammad's to consider whether a person deserves forgiveness. In fact, often we receive no apologies at all for the harm we perceive others to have caused since they're not even aware they have caused it.

It's hard to let feelings of unforgiveness go in situations like these. But doing so is crucial. If we don't, we risk harming the very people who have harmed us.

As we said in Chapter 3, unforgiveness is the root of all misbehavior. Unforgiveness compels us to lash out at our teammates, to verbally attack or emotionally abuse them, to become apathetic or disassociate from our jobs. Unfortunately, no form of misbehavior can release you from the hurt you are feeling. Sure, you might feel some temporary satisfaction by yelling at someone, but that satisfaction is fleeting. When it's gone, you're right back where you started—or maybe even worse off.

Viewed in this light, forgiveness isn't something we do for others but something we do for ourselves. It's a way to release ourselves from our pain, to overcome the grudges we hold, and to find peace both within ourselves and with those around us. One of the best approaches we've found to initiate forgiveness is service. When you serve the person who has caused you harm, you gain an opportunity to empathize and connect with that person—and eventually forgive them.

To be clear, this forgiveness may never be reciprocated. A teammate who doesn't know they've harmed you might also fail to recognize your effort to forgive them. At first glance, this might sound like a hard pill to swallow, but, in reality, it also doesn't matter. Even if the act of forgiveness is only for you and no one else, it's still worth the effort.

Less Time for Fighting, More Time for Innovation

Forgiveness improves trust and bolsters psychological safety. It also enables us to let go of our prison of unforgiveness and move forward with considerably less emotional baggage, fostering more agile, risk-tolerant teams. The greatest byproduct of forgiveness, then, is momentum.

This was why it was so important for Mohammad to ask his team in India for forgiveness. For nearly two years, Mohammad had done everything in his power to move the organization forward, but he'd struggled to create momentum with that effort until he admitted his mistakes and asked for his team's forgiveness.

It doesn't matter what initiative or process you introduce to get your company moving. Until you've identified and addressed the elephant in the room and asked for forgiveness—and until you've learned to forgive others without any expectation of reciprocity—all those efforts likely won't amount to much. Unforgiveness will still be simmering underneath everything that happens, eating away at your productivity, trust, and relationships.

A culture that actively practices forgiveness sees tremendous benefits in productivity, creativity, and innovation. When you lose fear, when you're unafraid of judgment or punishment, you feel empowered to take risks and think boldly.

Does everything work out perfectly 100 percent of the time? Absolutely not. However, a culture of love views failure as an opportunity, not as an embarrassing disaster that is just as quickly swept under the rug. In such an environment, we learn to forgive not only others for their perceived errors but ourselves as well.

Questions for "Forgiveness"

- ◆ Thinking about Mohammad's story at the beginning of this chapter, why is changing policy and process not enough to earn back trust and forgiveness?
- ◆ How often are you willing to ask for forgiveness at work? What's holding you back?
- ◆ What does it look like if forgiveness flows freely? How does that make you feel?
- ◆ How have you seen unforgiveness affect your workplace? How is that unforgiveness lived out?
- ◆ Thinking practically, how do you live out forgiveness in the workplace?

- How does accountability factor into forgiveness?
- Share a story about how you've embraced the power of apologizing at work. What happened as a result?
- Why do you think unforgiveness is so rampant in the workplace?
- Share a story about forgiveness and reconciliation in your workplace. What did you learn from that experience?
- How does forgiveness unlock or enhance the other pillars of love?
- Thinking practically, what can you start doing immediately to incorporate more forgiveness into the way you lead?
- After reading this chapter, are you skeptical about forgiveness in the workplace? If so, share those thoughts with the group.
- What were some of your biggest takeaways or *ah-ha* moments from this chapter?
- Share a moment of self-awareness about your leadership after reading this chapter.
- What, if anything, will you change or adjust about how you lead or behave based on what you've read?

Closing Out Part II

- When considering the Six Pillars of Love, which one do you find the most challenging to practice? Why?
- Which pillar is the easiest for you to embrace?
- Which pillar is missing from your organization the most? Why?
- Which pillar is the most important to achieve a healthy culture?
- What stories in Part II resonated with you the most? Why?
- How are you weaving the behaviors found in the Six Pillars into the way you lead? Share some practical steps you've taken to integrate them into how you behave.
- What lessons from Part II are you going to start incorporating in the way you lead others?

PART III

Put Love to Work

In Part I, we built the foundation. In Part II, we set up the pillars. Here in Part III, we're adding a roof.

Part III is for the tangible takeaways crowd. If that's you, thanks for being patient. We know this kind of action-oriented content is your bread and butter, but for everything to make sense, we had to lay some groundwork first.

In the chapters to come, we share our growth and transformation as an organization once we embraced a culture of love. We also put love to the test. Can "love" be woven into processes, tools, and hiring practices—the very DNA that makes a business functional? Is love really a *viable option* that can bridge the gap between better cultures and more revenue?

The answer—backed up with all the sweet, sweet data and insights you've been craving—is yes. And we're about to show you how it's possible.

One last thing before we start: Results take time. But, just as with exercise, gains are built and sustained over time. When you're in the middle of it, grinding it out every day, you may not even notice that you're making progress and packing muscle. Then, one day, you look in the mirror and realize that a whole new person is standing before you.

The point is, change often is felt before it's measured—but once it's measured, there won't be any room for doubt. Love can be your business strategy too.

CHAPTER 10

To Lead Is to Serve

It was around 2013. For nearly a decade, Softway had been relatively successful, but Mohammad was getting antsy. It was time for Softway to start attracting higher-profile clients and break into the big leagues.

So, he set a new goal: Grow the company past $50 million in revenue.

This was new territory for Mohammad. Looking for guidance, he sought out a new executive leadership team—industry vets who had helped oversee explosive growth at companies like IBM and Microsoft.

With an old-school sensibility about them, this new leadership team looked and acted the part of industry vets. More important to Mohammad, they had a plan for success—the same plan they had used for decades—and they expected everyone to follow it to the letter.

First things first. If he was going to lead a $50 million organization, the executive leadership team argued, Mohammad had to look and act the part. They gave him a set of rules to follow to "upgrade" his image:

- **Separate yourself from your employees.** Don't hang out with them on the floor. Let them know you are the boss and demand respect.

- **Dress and spend like a CEO.** Wear expensive suits, drive a fancy car, and spend lavishly. If that means buying a $150,000 Porsche on the company dime, then so be it.
- **Have a large, executive office that's separated from the rest of the company.** Preferably, this should be off in an executive wing, where employees won't feel comfortable walking through.
- **Never go to anyone with questions.** Make them come to you.

These rules had little to do with running a company. They were all about playing the part of CEO rather than *being* a CEO. To Mohammad, it all felt artificial.

But what did he know? For ten years, Mohammad had been going by his gut. These leaders had the bona fides—complete with impeccable resumes, fancy data, pie charts, and graphs. Even if Mohammad wanted to push back, he felt he had little wiggle room to do so. And so, Scrappy Startup Mohammad slowly transformed into CEO Mohammad.

No one particularly liked CEO Mohammad.

CEO Mohammad ignored his team members. CEO Mohammad wrote angry emails about refrigerator etiquette. CEO Mohammad expected that everyone would follow his ad hoc meeting schedule, their own calendars be damned.

For roughly three years, CEO Mohammad almost ran his company into the ground. It wasn't until he embraced Human Being Mohammad that Softway began to turn things around.

Granted, Human Being Mohammad wasn't immediately accepted either. Many leaders really *do* expect CEOs to look and act like CEO Mohammad had been. After Mohammad chose to break that mold, not everyone responded positively.

For instance, once Mohammad and another team member were at a meeting with a prospective client. Mohammad arrived at the meeting dressed casually in comfortable slacks and a nice sweater. As we later learned, after Mohammad left the team member to hammer out the specifics of the project, one of the VPs at the company protested. "I'm sorry, but is this really who we want to work with? Look at the way this guy dresses. Look at how he talks. He doesn't exactly scream *leadership material.*"

The company ultimately awarded Softway the contract—which we delivered on to the letter. Not long after, that same VP invited Mohammad to lunch, where he came clean about his initial reservations.

"Listen, Mohammad," the VP said. "I had this perception of you that was all wrong. I didn't think you carried yourself with the gravitas of a CEO, and we almost didn't give you our business because of it. Now I see what kind of leader you really are, and I just wanted to say that I'm glad I got to work with you. Thank you."

In that VP's transformation, Mohammad saw a reflection of his own. As a leader, it's easy to become too preoccupied with how we carry themselves, how our offices look, or what kinds of cars we drive. However, in a culture of love, leaders aren't focused on the trappings of their role but rather on how they *conduct* themselves—on which behaviors they bring to work, how they interact with others, and how they lead and inspire their teams.

In this chapter, we're going to share the story of Mohammad's transformational journey from traditional leadership to servant leadership. Before we do, we want to reiterate an important point. Leadership isn't just for the members of the C-suite. You don't have to be the CEO of your company to adopt the Ten Principles of Servant Leadership. No matter your position on the org chart, you can be a leader within your role. Although we use Mohammad's story to illustrate what servant leadership might look like, his is only one possible path. Your journey is your own. As we move through this story, we encourage you to take the lessons Mohammad learned, do some introspection, and apply instances of servant leadership that make sense to you in your leadership journey.

"What the Heck Is Servant Leadership?"

In 2015, only two weeks after Mohammad witnessed the University of Houston's miraculous comeback and began steering Softway toward a culture of love, a few of us had the opportunity to visit the Southwest Airlines headquarters in Dallas Love Field. We were excited about this visit for a couple of reasons. First, Southwest was interested in working with us. Second, a licensed pilot, Mohammad was thrilled to see all the planes on display at Southwest's corporate headquarters.

But as he walked the storied halls of Southwest Airlines, it wasn't the planes that caught his eye, but rather a big, attention-grabbing sign that read: SERVANT LEADERSHIP.

Wait, what the heck is servant leadership? Mohammad thought to himself.

Mohammad had never come across this term before, and he wasn't sure he understood its meaning. The words *servant* and *leader* together? It just didn't seem right.

Mohammad's understanding of *servant* was greatly influenced by Indian society, which has traditionally followed a tiered system. At the bottom, there are servants. At the top, there are leaders. And servants usually served the leaders. To Mohammad, the very idea of a "servant leader" was a contradiction. How could someone possibly be both at the same time?

Still, Mohammad was curious. So he began doing some research. As he discovered, servant leadership is a philosophy and set of practices in which leaders put the needs of the team before themselves to create an environment where the team can be successful. As the Greenleaf Center for Servant Leadership says, "Servant leadership enriches the lives of individuals, builds better organizations, and ultimately creates a more just and caring world."[1]

The more Mohammad learned, the more he understood why Southwest Airlines had displayed that banner so prominently. In many ways, Southwest's embrace of servant leadership is the difference between its famously excellent customer experience and the not-so-good experiences found at other airlines. Southwest paints hearts on its planes, its employees actually smile, and it refuses to deceive people with nickel-and-dime charges on top of fares. It also takes customer dissatisfaction seriously and acts quickly to resolve any problems.

Servant leadership isn't just a fad at Southwest Airlines. It's what led the company to become profitable for the forty-six straight years through 2020. Southwest's cofounder and former CEO, Herb Kelleher, actively practiced servant leadership—hanging out with his team, spearheading culture initiatives, and even jumping in to help lighten the load of the baggage crew.

Mohammad's discovery of servant leadership couldn't have come at a better moment. This philosophy was a natural fit for the culture of love he was trying to build at Softway, and Southwest offered the perfect example of how to put this practice in action.

From that moment on, Mohammad was all in. No more putting himself first as a leader. No more obsessing over appearances. His number-one duty was to serve others, to create a safe environment for his team, and to remove any barriers to their success. And that was exactly what he was going to do.

A culture of love is enabled and embodied through servant leadership. This practice is not just a nice thing to have. It is essential.

The Ten Principles of Servant Leadership

Servant leadership doesn't come with an on/off switch. Mohammad didn't just learn about servant leadership one day, decide to do it, and then never think about it again. Servant leadership is a journey with no destination—and one that Mohammad is still on today.

Of course, before he could even get started on this journey, first he had to mend all the bridges that CEO Mohammad had burned. This was no small task. Mohammad's chronic misbehaviors had created significant mistrust and unforgiveness, and it took him years to regain his organization's trust. Although at times he worried that the damage he had caused might be irreversible, he was determined to try anyway.

The Principles of Servant Leadership are time-tested and battle-worn. The journey of servant leadership might be long and uncertain, but these principles will help you start off on the right foot.

PRINCIPLE #1: PUT OTHERS' NEEDS FIRST

For years, the needs of CEO Mohammad came before anyone else's. Softway team members knew this all too well, which is why many initially dismissed Mohammad's embrace of servant leadership. We tried to explain the value of this new approach—and that our own needs would take a backseat to theirs—but our words went in one ear and out the other.

But as the old cliché goes, actions speak louder than words. It was one thing to *say* that we wanted to put team members' needs before our own, but it was another thing to do it. The problem was, we didn't know our team members' needs. Team members were so jaded after so many years of abuse that they wouldn't open up to us.

Here is where our empathy pillar becomes so important: No matter how we fit in an organization, our lives are rich and nuanced. Whatever someone thinks you are like on the surface, there's always more going on behind the scenes. As leaders, we should never assume we know what people are dealing with.

Instead, we should put in the work and find out. Ask questions. Engage. Learn about your team members. If you suspect there's a problem lurking under the surface, don't ignore it—dive in and uncover it.

If Mohammad wanted his team members to open up, he had to prove his sincerity. So he moved out of his big, fancy CEO office and into the bullpen so he could work side by side with his team. No more awkward walks through the executive suite. If his team members needed something, he would be right there to help them.

Being in the bullpen also made Mohammad more visible—really, really visible. For the next year, he was the first person to show up and the last person to leave. If other team members were staying late, he would order them dinner. Whatever it took to be present and supportive, he would do it. Through every action, Mohammad embodied the principle of putting others' needs before his own.

PRINCIPLE #2: BE HUMBLE AND PRACTICE GRATITUDE

Be humble enough to learn and vulnerable enough to apologize. During the CEO Mohammad years, Mohammad never once wrote a thank-you note. Not one.

Human Being Mohammad went all in on gratitude, sending out personalized, handwritten notes to everyone in the office. For instance, if a team member was quietly putting in long hours, Mohammad wrote them a note to recognize their effort. Often these notes would come with gift cards—a subtle nudge to the team member to take a night off every once in a while and take their family to dinner.

Not only did Mohammad want his team members to feel noticed, but he also wanted them to know he wasn't above them. For years, every time he traveled to our India office, he only made time to meet with leadership. He saw no reason to speak with anyone else.

After his embrace of servant leadership, however, that changed. Now when he traveled to India, he spoke with everyone—including the janitorial staff. He made it a point to take team members out to meals and to learn about their lives, families, and ambitions. With over a hundred team members in India, this meant a lot of meals over a five-day trip. So, while he always came back to Houston a little heavier, he also came back a lot more fulfilled.

He also often came back with gifts for his Houston team. On one trip, for instance, he brought back Indian bangles and anklets for the women in the office and Indian shirts (or *kurtas*) for the men. But he didn't stop there; Mohammad also brought back gifts for team members' kids as well.

Why did Mohammad go to all this trouble—and how was he able to fit so many gifts into his luggage? Because he wanted to demonstrate gratitude through action, to show that he was thinking about them and that he cared about their well-being. On his journey to becoming a servant leader, his team had given him the gift of feedback (even if that feedback was hard to hear). To show his appreciation and to demonstrate humility for what his team had done for him, bringing along a few gifts was the least he could do.

As for the luggage question, that remains a mystery. A leader has to keep *some* secrets, after all.

PRINCIPLE #3: DO NOT ASK OTHERS TO DO SOMETHING THAT YOU ARE NOT WILLING TO DO

Before a servant leader asks someone to do something, they're prepared to do it themselves. They know all contributions are worthwhile. No matter how small or menial, no task is beneath them. In other words, small actions speak volumes. If you expect your employees to clean up after each other or make a new pot of coffee, then you must be willing to do those things as well.

If you sweat the little things, then your team will too. By serving his employees food, cleaning the office, and giving them rides, Mohammad demonstrated servant leadership in action. But he didn't stop there. He also made it a point to learn and perform every role in the company. (See Chapter 8.) To better serve his team, he needed to understand their experiences.

Through this effort, Mohammad learned *a lot*. For instance, when he took on the role of project manager, he struggled. All the different processes were simply too much to keep up with. But Mohammad couldn't complain. After all, *he* was the one who put those processes in place. If he couldn't do the job himself, then he had no business asking his project managers to do it either.

PRINCIPLE #4: ASSUME GOOD INTENT

Prior to 2016, Softway had installed biometric scanners in our offices. We said that the scanners enhanced security (and that was true), but we also used them to track employee movements. We knew exactly when they arrived at work and exactly when they left. If they showed up late or left early, we docked their pay. (For the full story, see Chapter 13.)

After shifting to a culture of love, we dismantled this system as part of our campaign to reestablish trust among our teams. The problem wasn't with the system itself, of course. It was with our motivation for using it.

Simply put, CEO Mohammad didn't trust his employees. He assumed bad intent in every action, convinced that team members were constantly trying to get one over on us and get paid for doing nothing. The biometric system was emblematic of that distrust, and its influence could be felt throughout the organization. Eventually just about everyone had adopted the same pessimistic outlook as Mohammad.

In business theory, an authoritarian company that assumes the bad intent of all its employees is known as a *Theory X* organization. For instance, if a policy is being abused, the organization will remove or amend that policy. Today Softway takes a *Theory Y* approach. We are a participative organization that assumes that all our team members operate with good intent. If a policy is being abused, we address the issue with the offenders rather than punish the entire organization.

This wasn't an easy transition. Sometimes it was difficult to break old habits. In fact, doing so required us to go against our very nature. As humans, when we see someone make a choice that we disagree with, our first impulse is to assume that person is acting in bad faith. In fact, usually the opposite is true. People generally operate in good faith.

We've learned firsthand that assuming good intent takes active practice—which is precisely what makes it such an important part of servant leadership. It doesn't matter whether you're in a conversation in the hallway, participating in a meeting, or learning about a choice someone made that didn't work out. When you assume good intent, you approach that moment with genuine trust and empathy. As a result, you're far more willing to see the situation from the other person's perspective (and nullify all those misbehaviors we outlined in Chapter 3). It's hard to turn inward and feel persecuted when you're focused on your team members' perspective rather than your own.

PRINCIPLE #5: LOOK FOR THE GOOD IN OTHERS AND FIND THE WEAKNESSES IN YOURSELF

This principle works in lockstep with Principle #4. Not only should you assume good intent, but you should also focus on the positives in others rather than dwell on any of the negatives.

For instance, Mohammad knew that, in order to embody a culture of love, he would have to learn to love his team. Such behavior didn't come naturally for him—how can you love your team when you're so focused on all their mistakes and bad behaviors? Finally one of Mohammad's mentors helped him look for their good qualities rather than look for the bad.

In our personal lives, this is easy for most of us to do. In a loving relationship, we're more than willing to look past the bad and focus on the good. Servant leaders understand that there's no reason our working relationships can't operate in the same way. Our role is to bring out the best in our teams, not highlight their worst. If someone makes a mistake or if their bad qualities begin to shine through, we must be willing to look past these misbehaviors to see all the good qualities too.

At the same time, we must also be on the lookout for our own misbehaviors. After all, servant leaders have weaknesses too. Through constant introspection and self-awareness, you can identify your flaws and work to become a better leader.

That said, whatever flaws you uncover, don't be too hard on yourself. Nobody's perfect. We're all always under construction. Sure, you might misbehave or make mistakes from time to time, but don't forget all the good you're capable of too.

PRINCIPLE #6: RESPOND INSTEAD OF REACT

Imagine you're in a crowded restaurant with your family. All of a sudden, a cockroach appears on the table. Everyone screams. You leap from the table, frantically swatting at the cockroach, but it flies off and lands on another table—sending that group into a frenzy too. The cockroach escapes again, this time landing on another unsuspecting diner's back. Then, before this hapless diner can react, a waiter calmly walks over, grabs the cockroach, and tosses it outside.

Feeling squeamish yet?

Don't worry, this is all hypothetical. No diners (or cockroaches) were harmed in the telling of this story.

Here's the moral of the story: While the customers at the first two tables *reacted,* the waiter *responded*—and that distinction made all the difference.

When we only react to situations, chaos usually follows. And where there's chaos, there's misbehavior. We blow up, we exaggerate the issue, and we fail to assume good intent.

Like the waiter, servant leaders *respond.* They are calm in the face of challenges. They consider all parties involved and then choose the best course of action available to them. And when they don't respond as well as they could have, they own up to it.

PRINCIPLE #7: KNOW THAT POWER DOES NOT EQUAL LEADERSHIP

If you've never had the privilege of flying from Houston to Bengaluru, you're missing out. . .on about twenty-seven hours of travel on a one-stop flight (if you're lucky). It's a bit of an ordeal, one that Mohammad and other members of Softway's Houston team make about four times a year.

For years, although Mohammad would fly business class, the rest of the team would fly economy. It was easy to justify this disparity from a business perspective. Mohammad flew more often, business class was expensive, and Mohammad was the CEO. Sure, he felt guilty about it, but he wasn't prepared to do anything about it.

Eventually Mohammad realized that's not how a servant leader would act. So he began flying economy with the rest of the Houston crew. To his surprise, it wasn't that bad. It might have even been an upgrade! Mohammad loved connecting with the rest of his team and strengthening those relationships.

That said, there were challenges. Everyone enjoyed seeing more of Mohammad, but not everyone enjoyed sitting next to him. As Chris will be the first to tell you, Mohammad has what he affectionately calls sleep tremors. There's nothing scary or dangerous about them. It's just that he twitches and jabs a lot. If you're sitting next to Mohammad while he sleeps, you're going to end up with some bruised ribs—and you won't get a wink of sleep yourself.

Sleep is important when you're flying halfway around the world, but flying economy made that difficult. Team members were arriving in Houston or Bengaluru jet-lagged and exhausted—and their jam-packed schedules offered them little chance to catch up on any sleep. After experiencing these struggles, Mohammad made sure everyone got to fly business class as soon as Softway could afford it. It was a larger expense (business class tickets generally run five times higher than economy class), but it was the right thing to do.

PRINCIPLE #8: TAKE CARE OF OTHERS (WHO IN TURN WILL TAKE CARE OF YOU)

During Softway's most desperate days, we had over seven figures in debt, our credit line was maxed out, and we were behind on rent for our office. When Mohammad asked, "Will we be able to open our doors tomorrow?," it wasn't hyperbole.

As bleak as things looked, Mohammad vowed that as long as his team was fighting to keep the company in business, he would fight to keep them employed. This meant pulling out all the stops:

◆ He mortgaged his fully paid-off home to make payroll.

◆ He sold his Porsche and put the money back into the company. His new ride became Softway's 2011 Toyota Sienna minivan. (He has since upgraded to a newer Toyota Sienna minivan and is very proud of his "minivan dad" status.)

◆ He stopped taking a paycheck for eight months so his employees could get paid.

His sacrifices didn't go unnoticed. By putting others' needs before his own, Mohammad inspired the rest of his team to go all in for the company as well. Executives in both our American and Indian offices took pay cuts to help out, including Jeff, who declined all pay for two months. Some team members—for example, our financial controller, Taban—declined a salary entirely until Mohammad started taking one for himself again. (Taban also conspired with Jeff to keep the latter's refusal of salary a secret.) Many on the sales team gave up commissions and bonuses to make sure the company remained solvent.

As Mohammad's spirit of sacrifice trickled through the company, the culture began to transform. Despite the hard times, morale was high. Buoyed by this spirit, Softway began to turn things around.

PRINCIPLE #9: INCLUSION AND BELONGING BEGIN WITH SERVANT LEADERSHIP

Up to this point, Principles #1 to #8 have all been leading to the same place: inclusion. If you are committed to creating an environment of inclusion within your organization, then servant leadership is the first step on the path. Without putting the needs of others before yourself, without practicing gratitude, without assuming good intent in others, there is no inclusion. Period.

Here is the greatest contrast between traditional leadership and servant leadership. Traditional leadership states that everything should revolve around the leader, which is a fundamentally passive approach. Servant leadership requires active participation—to speak with your team, hear what they have to say, invite their input, and consider their ideas. Enabling someone to feel heard is one of the best ways for them to grow. The more each individual team member is able to grow, the more your organization will grow along with them. Servant leaders create space and access to make this happen.

PRINCIPLE #10: CHANGE STARTS WITH YOU

For over a decade, Mohammad operated with the mindset that others should be working *for* him, not *with* him. Fortunately, just before this mindset nearly sank Softway, Mohammad had an epiphany that changed the company—and our team—for the better.

This change had to start with Mohammad. As the CEO, he was the one creating the playbook for the company. To spark change, first he had to change himself.

You don't need to be a CEO to practice this or any other principle of servant leadership. Anyone can embody the change they want to see in their organization. If you're in a toxic environment at your company, break the cycle and commit to change. Assume the good intentions of those around you and ask yourself how you can better serve them. This change won't happen overnight, but here's the good thing: It's contagious. The more we work to improve the lives of those around us, the more likely others are to do the same.

Being Okay with Tough Times

Softway has come a long way from the days of CEO Mohammad. For years he followed the advice of an executive leadership team that was well intentioned but operating from an outdated playbook written during a different era.

To gain an advantage in a competitive world, we learned that we could no longer operate in this outmoded mindset. So, to create high-performing teams, we committed to serving those teams by making each person feel like a valued, important part of a well-oiled machine.

That said, a warning: Although servant leadership is essential to a culture of love, the path can be a lonely one. Servant leadership means supporting those you lead—often without being seen. As such, it can be a quiet and thankless task. There will be tough days, days when no one notices your work or thanks you for what you're doing to help them succeed. You will rarely have opportunities for public recognition—and you will have *zero* opportunities to brag.

That's the nature of the work, and you must be okay with it.

Of course, perhaps even more challenging than the days when no one notices your work are the days when *everyone* notices—the days when you make a big, obvious mistake. Leaders are only human. We screw up just like everyone else. However, when *we* screw up, we're held to a higher standard. Every single move, every single behavior, every single action we take (or don't take) will be critiqued, judged, and second-guessed. Even if you make only one mistake in a sea of otherwise perfect behavior, you still will be judged for that one mistake. And you must be okay with it.

No matter how much good you've done or how much goodwill you might have built up, those moments can send your company back a mile or more. And it will be your job to turn around, pick up the pieces, and start over. These are the moments in which others form their perceptions of you, and these perceptions will become their reality. You must be okay with that too.

As a servant leader, you will be expected to have empathy toward your team members and always do the best for your team, even if your team may not always do the same for you. You will be expected to understand the personal needs of your team members and what they may be experiencing in their personal lives, even if your team may not do the same for you. Finally, you will be expected to trust your team absolutely, even if they do not always show the same trust in you. In all those situations too, you must be okay with it.

There is no fairness in leadership. Often you will have to work harder than those around you. This effort will be a lot of responsibility to shoulder, but know this: The sacrifices, the tough times, and the difficulties you go through as a leader *will* show results—and, eventually, your efforts *will* be noticed.

How do we know? Because every organization is a reflection of the leaders who build it, piece by piece, day after day. As a leader, your behaviors have an outsize impact on your culture. Every choice you make is an opportunity to build that culture up or tear it down. *You* set the tone—and for better or worse, others will follow.

In that regard, every time someone celebrates your culture, every time someone celebrates a big win, every time someone shares how happy they are to be doing work that matters, remember that they're celebrating *you* as well.

These are the moments we all aspire to as leaders. But to get there, remember this: You cannot expect your culture or anyone around you to develop faster than you do as a leader. You must go first and set the tone for others to follow. If you can do that, then you can become a principal driver of a culture of love.

Questions for "To Lead Is to Serve"

- ◆ What leadership myths have you believed that turned out to be false?
- ◆ What rules of leadership could be antithetical to a culture of love?
- ◆ How would you define *servant leadership*?
- ◆ What are some potential drawbacks of servant leadership?
- ◆ Out of the Ten Principles of Servant Leadership, which one impacted you the most?
- ◆ Explain why.
- ◆ Which principle is the hardest to put into practice? Why?
- ◆ What's holding you back from embracing servant leadership?
- ◆ Have you experienced the loneliness that Mohammad described as part of this style of leadership?
- ◆ Thinking practically, what can you do today to incorporate servant leadership principles into the way you lead?
- ◆ After reading this chapter, are you skeptical about servant leadership in the workplace? If so, share those thoughts with the group.
- ◆ What were some of your biggest takeaways or *ah-ha* moments from this chapter?
- ◆ Share a moment of self-awareness about your leadership after reading this chapter.
- ◆ What, if anything, will you change or adjust about the way you lead or behave based on what you've read?

Note

1. www.greenleaf.org

CHAPTER 11

We Are Better Together

Your palms are sweaty, knees weak, arms heavy (something about Mom's spaghetti). Your heart is beating a hundred miles an hour, your face is flushed, and you can barely breathe.

There is a bomb in front of you. It is counting down. . .four minutes and ten seconds until it blows up the building. All around you, people are scrambling to evacuate. Unless you can defuse it, at least two dozen people will be harmed in the blast.

There's just one problem: You don't know the first thing about bombs.

Luckily, the team of experts speaking to you over the intercom does. As long as you can relay the right information back and forth, you and everyone else just may survive.

Do you feel like you're in a James Bond film yet?

Spoiler alert: There's no real bomb. It's all just a simulation.

We've led this bomb game exercise with thousands of leaders over the years—many of whom are established vets with twenty or thirty years of experience. In terms of individual performance, these leaders are the cream of the crop. However, when we ask them to work together to defuse this bomb, most of them are unable to do so.

Failure, of course, is the point of the game. We want to illustrate the difference between how potentially high-performing teams *could* operate and how they often do. Nothing about this challenge is especially difficult:

- One person sits across the room from the rest of the team. Only this "technician" can see the bomb.
- The "experts" sit on the other side of the room. Only they have the instructions for diffusing the bomb, which are written in simple words on a black-and-white page.
- The experts must communicate those instructions to the technician across the room.
- Together, they have five minutes and several steps to complete to save the day.

It's a tense exercise—one made more so with a live audience watching and following along. But if you keep your cool and communicate, you should be able to get through it.

Some teams do. We've learned that these teams all share a few common elements:

- They feel free to speak up.
- They will admit ignorance and describe what they do or do not know quickly.
- There is no single leader in the group.
- Team members take turns leading and sharing what they have learned.

Contrast that with the teams that blew up the bomb, ran out of time, or both. These teams often share some common traits as well:

- They start by sitting heads down, staring at the manual.
- They hardly speak to each other, often because they're either scared or worried they might disrupt what's going on around them.
- There is no trust between the person defusing the bomb and the teammates reading the manual. The person controlling the bomb will describe what they see but won't trust what they hear back.

You can hear this distrust in the way they talk to each other:

"Cut the fourth wire."

"The fourth from the top counting down?"

"Uhhhh—yes."

"It's a yellow wire. Is that okay?"

"I. . .think so. Do it."

"Are you sure?"

"Pretty sure. Go ahead."

The technician cuts the wire. The team has arrived at the right answer, but their overcommunication is eating up time. At this pace, they will lose.

Now, to be fair, it's okay to be a little cautious when defusing a bomb. This is an (imaginary) life-or-death situation, after all. But here's the thing: It's okay to make some mistakes. If you cut the wrong wire, you don't automatically lose the game You get three chances. The teams that fail ignore this fact, unwilling to make even a single mistake.

The successful teams, in contrast, trust each other—even enough to make mistakes.

"Cut the fourth wire."

"Oh. That was wrong."

"Okay, what happened?"

"I see what I did. I think it's the yellow one. Should I try that one instead?"

"Actually, yes, I think the yellow one is right."

"Okay. It's cut."

"Great! Now I need you to find the green button."

See the difference? The team may have made a mistake, but it also made progress. While the mistrusting team is still trying to sort out the first step, the trusting team is already onto the third one.

Now, you and your teams probably don't defuse bombs as part of your jobs (unless you work for a bomb squad, in which case, we salute you). You probably don't work on a five-minute timer either, and you probably can see what everyone else on your team is doing.

Still, there's a difference between successful and unsuccessful teams. Successful teams trust each other in all directions, often without question. They demonstrate empathy through listening, are open to each other's feedback, make fast friends, and solve problems collaboratively.

Unsuccessful teams, in contrast, get hung up on process and tools, fear of failure, and power dynamics. As a result, they forget their common goal—in this case, making sure the room doesn't explode. Many teams with VP-level executives will literally freeze until the most "powerful" person makes the first move. Instead of playing the bomb game, all their mental energy is focused on playing a totally different game of politics.

This minute of silence and inaction in the game is equivalent to a month of silence during a large project. Everyone is focused on learning their job and looking good in front of the boss, and no one is communicating. For the next few months, no one takes any initiative. It's all back-and-forth messages and second-guessing. Before you know it, four months have gone by, nothing has been accomplished, and there's only one month left to complete five months of work.

When team members don't trust each other, the bomb explodes—whether figuratively or literally. In this chapter, we're going to teach you how to build expert, empathetic bomb squads. In other words, we're going to teach you how to create a high-performing team that is aligned with a culture of love.

The Five Traits of a High-Performing Team

Here's a question to kick things off: What exactly is a high-performing team? Organizations (ours included) love to throw this term around, but its meaning can vary.

We define a high-performing team as a team that regularly exceeds expectations. In our experience, these teams exhibit these five traits:

1. **Autonomous.** Team members work with limited oversight. They collaborate and self-prioritize efficiently, and link their work to clear outcomes and goals.

2. **Six-pillar culture.** Team members care for one another and hold one another accountable, representing all Six Pillars of Love: inclusion, trust, empowerment, vulnerability, empathy, and forgiveness.

3. **"We" is greater than "I."** As we said earlier, it's better to have an all-star team than a team of all stars. The members of high-performing teams are motivated to help each other rather than by self-interest. They pay attention to their teammates' needs and engage with empathy. They don't compete against each other but rather against forces outside the team or company.

4. **Outcomes oriented.** Fearful of looking bad or embarrassing themselves, low- or average-performing teams tend deliver only what is asked of them, even if they know better. A high-performing team, by contrast, delivers what is *needed*, not what is requested.

5. **Fine with failure.** High-performing teams approach failure with a growth mindset. They see failure not as a destination but as an opportunity to learn and improve.

Do these traits describe your team? If so, then you are probably part of a high-performing team. Congratulations! At Softway, we *thought* we had several high-performing teams, but, in reality, we did not. How do we know? Well, let's just say a lot more teams bombed the bomb game than we expected.

Ultimately, the defining trait of a high-performing team is risk tolerance. A risk-averse team's fear of failure eats up more time than the failure itself, causing very to get little done. Risk-tolerant teams, however, are more vulnerable, openly share and discuss ideas, and experience greater comfort and camaraderie. So how do you create high-performing, risk-tolerant teams? That's what the rest of this chapter is all about.

Create Psychological Safety

In Chapter 1, we shared the story of Amy Edmondson and her research on how working teams of doctors and nurses interacted.

Much to her surprise, Edmondson found that high-performing doctor/nurse teams talked about their failures most often.

Edmondson also examined the role of teamwork during the operation to rescue a group of thirty-three stranded Chilean miners in 2010. To free the trapped miners, leaders assembled a diverse team of experts, including black ops, NASA, and geology. Despite their diverse backgrounds and expertise, the team members communicated surprisingly well with each other. The geologist didn't insist she was right because she was the geologist. The special ops military person didn't insist he was right because he'd conducted rescue missions before. Everyone was willing to add ideas together until they found the solution as a group.[1]

So what was their secret? Why were they able to communicate with each other and execute so effectively? In short, before setting out to solve the problem at hand, the team members worked to establish psychological safety within the group. Each person agreed they were there to solve the same problem—and that everyone's contribution was important and deserved to be heard. No one dominated the conversation, and everyone had a chance to contribute.

You may not realize it, but your organization and the teams within it are composed of an equally diverse group of role players— project managers, analysts, engineers, designers, and so on. The stakes may not be as high as defusing a bomb or rescuing a group of miners, but you still need to work together in order to reach your goal.

To create psychological safety among your teams, prioritize these behaviors:

- **Team members ask questions.** If Chris doesn't understand something about a given project, he asks. He's not afraid of being judged or criticized, so he has no reason to keep any questions to himself. Further, he knows that by asking questions, he helps the team to consider the project from multiple angles, anticipate problems, and improve their approach.
- **Team members engage others.** If Jeff and Frank are trying to solve a problem and they notice Mohammad has disengaged,

they work to get Mohammad back on the problem. Sometimes that means talking an issue out, and sometimes that means giving Mohammad space for a moment. Either way, the solution starts by acknowledging the problem and stating your desire to move past it.

◆ **Team members forgive.** Jeff and Frank don't get mad at Mohammad for checking out. Mohammad is only human, and no one can remain engaged 100 percent of the time. Speaking around problems only slows down progress. Forgiveness and reconciliation remove the sticky parts and keep the team moving forward.

Every organization wants to create high-performing teams, but they ignore the critical first step of creating psychological safety. Instead, the person who has the most experience, the most seniority, or the most education commands outsize influence on the problem solving and decision-making process. This *intellectual arrogance,* to borrow a term, usually leads to low-performing teams. Why? Because all those other people in the room who don't have the best job title or the most impressive degree are afraid to raise their hands and contribute—even if they're certain they can answer the problem. How much lived experience and wisdom could be translated into innovation in corporations, if only it were heard?

Destroying Safety

Psychological safety is much easier to destroy than it is to create. If you are focused on building psychological safety, don't be afraid to exercise authoritative power and call out any destructive behaviors quickly and unambiguously.

We've all seen the kinds of behaviors that alienate others: talking over other people, not inviting people to meetings they should be part of, spellchecking out loud, interrupting presentations, asking questions the person already knows the answers to, and so on. Manipulative, passive-aggressive misbehaviors,

(continued)

and other mind games are death to psychological safety, and the marginalization these actions create cannot be tolerated.

Sometimes a team member might use overtly hostile, destructive language. Or they might approach a problem with intellectual arrogance, ignoring others' suggestions because their education or job title doesn't "merit" the attention. Whatever the case, if you notice a psychologically unsafe behavior, bring attention to it immediately by offering feedback or by practicing healthy authoritative power. Try not to respond with anger or hostility, but instead offer your feedback as a gift.

To take a more active role in a healthy working environment, download our pre-meeting psychological safety checklist at www.LoveAsAStrategy.com/resources.

Communication and Expectations

What style of feedback should we use?
How do we want to practice accountability?
How should we discuss workload?

Effective expectation-setting means answering as many of these questions as you can up front, but it's never too late to take a moment to recenter and make sure everyone understands and learns from each other. To guide your effort, we recommend establishing working agreements—team-generated series of statements that promote accountability and keep everyone aligned.

At Softway, we practice a direct, efficient, and clear style of communication in all situations. Think back to Chapter 1, when Maggie directly and unambiguously confronted Chris for no-showing to their meeting. Sure, addressing the issue head on meant Chris felt a little sheepish for the next few days, but it also brought Maggie's concerns out into the open quickly rather than letting them fester.

This approach to communication is the standard to which all teams should aspire. When defusing bombs, there's simply no time for fluff. Open and honest conversations allow our teams to align, provide us with a blueprint for how to resolve disputes before they happen, and help us solve problems collaboratively.

With that said, do not mistake directness for cruelty. Our particular communication style might be effective for us, but it might fall flat in other organizations. Think of your working agreement as a positive prenup. In any group of people, something always will go wrong. However you define it, a working agreement can set expectations and make issues much easier to address when they do arise.

Accountability

The word *accountability* makes people nervous. They think of accountability in terms of deliverables. Did they get that assignment in on time? Did they remember to send off that email? Did they get the order for the team lunch right?

This is what accountability looks like in low-performing teams. It's rooted in authoritative and punitive power and reinforces ideas of hierarchy. Sometimes it gets results, but typically it doesn't work very well. And it certainly won't work in a culture of love.

When we think of the principles of accountability in a high-performing team, here's what we mean:

- Stand with your teammates—for them, with them, alongside them. Whatever they do, you do.
- Uphold high standards of performance and expectations so that everyone can achieve them.
- Speak up, even if you're disappointed or frustrated.
- Don't offer feedback as a personal attack but rather as an invitation to help the team improve.

To understand what accountability in a culture of love looks like, think back to Chapter 3, when Frank held Mohammad accountable for his misbehavior over a missed but not really missed meeting. Frank was deeply hurt and frustrated over the experience, but he communicated that frustration and held Mohammad accountable in a way that invited improvement rather than stoked conflict.

Giving Feedback

Imagine Jeff has just handed you a gift—or at least, he said it was a gift. Honestly, it looks like trash. The box is wrapped in newspaper with strips of randomly colored duct tape topped off with some twine that kinda resembles a bow. You take Jeff's gift, thank him for the consideration, and then set it down. *Whatever that is, it can wait.*

Then Chris hands you a gift. It looks and feels amazing—nice, shiny paper perfectly tucked and folded, with six-inch ribbon curls trailing down like icing on a cake. Truly, he is a gifted gift wrapper. Impressed, you open Chris's gift right away and look inside to find your favorite new card game: Throw Throw Burrito. (Look it up. It's a real game, and it's fantastic.)

Then you turn back to Jeff's gift. You sigh. *If a squirrel jumps out at me, I'm going to lose it,* you think. You unlace the twine, peel off a strip of duct tape, and unwrap the newspaper to find. . .another copy of Throw Throw Burrito!

Would you look at that? Two wildly different wrapping jobs. *Exactly the same gift.*

Giving feedback is a lot like giving a gift: You can wrap it up however you like, but the only thing that matters is what's inside. Sure, someone might be more receptive to hearing feedback if you wrapped it up better. But even if it's not nicely wrapped, you've still shared something incredibly valuable—the gift of someone else's perspective.

At Softway, we're big gift givers—both in terms of actual gifts and the gift of feedback. Because we love each other and care about everyone's success, we want to give them the best opportunity to succeed. After all, we're all human. We all misbehave and fall short of expectations. We all need to have hard conversations. That's okay. As long as your team is built on a strong foundation of psychological safety, these conversations can be incredibly valuable and impactful to your team's performance.

So why do we put such a premium on gift giving? Because we've learned that teams that give good gifts grow far beyond teams that don't. The more you exercise your gift-giving muscle, the better you get. The more you avoid gift giving, the more tortured and laborious the process becomes. You don't need to be a Chris-level gift wrapper to offer valuable feedback to your teammate. You just need to know what good feedback looks like.

HOW TO GIVE BAD FEEDBACK

You've just kicked off a one-on-one meeting with Frank. Before you dive into the conversation, Frank says, "Hey, just so you know, you had spinach in your teeth all day yesterday."

"Thanks?" you say. You know that Frank was just trying to be nice, but it sure would have been more helpful if he'd told you that yesterday.

You probably get the point of this story. Good feedback is actionable; bad feedback is not. You can't get the spinach out of your teeth today if you don't learn about it until tomorrow.

To avoid your own Frank moment, practice giving feedback in real time. Don't wait for the perfect situation. Don't curate the perfect playlist, light the candles, and set the mood. The longer you wait, the less relevant the feedback becomes, and the less opportunity the person has to learn. Besides, the sooner you give the feedback, the sooner it's over with.

Untimely feedback isn't the only way to give bad feedback, of course. Here are a few other things to avoid:

- **Unfounded gossip.** Just because you heard Peter was having trouble with his TPS reports doesn't make it true. Before offering any feedback, make sure you have your facts straight.
- **Playing the messenger.** Here's a sure sign you're giving bad feedback: "Hey, I just wanted you to know—and it's not me saying this—but Mohammad was saying that he's tired of the 'science project'—his words, not mine—that you left in the refrigerator. Do you think you can do something about that?" How awkward. Your feedback needs to come from you. Don't hide behind someone else.
- **A chance to misbehave.** As it turns out, you didn't actually have spinach in your teeth. Frank was just acting shady. If your goal in giving feedback isn't to help someone but rather to attack, belittle, or play mind games with that person, then that's not feedback. That's misbehavior.

There are other ways to give bad feedback—too many to list in this book. But, big picture, if you're not sure how to deliver feedback, start with one of our Ten Principles of Servant Leadership, as described in Chapter 10: Assume good intent.

HOW TO GIVE GOOD FEEDBACK

We were in a client meeting, about to make a pivotal decision, when our client pushed back hard. Suddenly, all the air went out of the room, and Mohammad shut down.

Feeling the awkward silence swell around him, Frank looked up from his laptop. This bad vibe couldn't continue. They were there to serve their client, and right now, they weren't doing it.

Frank waited a few moments for someone else to speak up. After all, offering real-time feedback wasn't his favorite thing to do. He was perfectly happy sitting there behind his laptop, thank you very much.

But as the awkwardness dragged on, Frank concluded that no one else was going to say anything. It was up to him. So, he closed his laptop, cleared his throat, and said: "I want everybody to stop for a quick minute, please."

Everyone stopped what they were doing and turned toward Frank.

He continued. "Mohammad, I noticed that you shut down in the conversation just now, and that cannot happen. We're at a pivotal moment. What can we do to bring you back into the conversation and help us make this decision?"

Instead of giving the feedback later—or even offering it one-on-one away from the client—Frank chose to address the issue immediately. The clients were literally paying to be there in the room, and he wanted to set the right tone.

This approach wasn't without risks, of course. Mohammad could have responded negatively after Frank called attention to him. But even though Frank *hated* confrontation, this wasn't his first rodeo. He knew how to give good feedback. To bring his teammate back into the conversation, he directly asked Mohammad what he needed. Rather than focus on a critique, he focused on actions. As a result, Mohammad was able to consider his own needs, get clarity, and rejoin the conversation. The rest of the room followed suit. Once everyone was ready to reengage as a group, Mohammad was able to move through the rest of his presentation without a hitch.

Offering feedback in the moment often feels awkward, especially in a group setting. But many times, as was the case in this situation, things were awkward already. Better to lean into the awkwardness, call it out, and work to resolve it than to let it fester. By creating an opportunity for everyone to move past the awkwardness, the team was able to come back together around a shared goal and continue to move forward.

Create a Path to Action

Imagine if one of your teammates walked up to you and said that you were hard to talk to during meetings. How would you feel? Probably pretty embarrassed—and probably at a loss as to how to improve your behavior.

In moments like that, the gift of feedback is all wrapping and no present, and it's not even that good of a wrapping job.

If you want to make sure you include a present with your gift, offer clear, actionable feedback. Even if you don't wrap the present very well, most of the time your teammates will recognize the offering and thank you for it.

That said, if you can, take care to wrap your feedback as well as you can. Follow the Platinum Rule. (See Chapter 5.) Take a moment to understand what your teammate needs and how you can best help them get there.

The Role of Leaders on a High-Performing Team

In the bomb game, if you screw up and clip the wrong wire, there are no real consequences. In business, setting off a figurative bomb could have far-reaching consequences for your organization. But whether in the bomb game or at work, mistakes are going to happen. The question is, how do you and your team respond? Do you watch as your team shuts down and flies into a panic? Or does someone step in to pick everyone up, reorient the team, and keep pushing ahead?

In a culture of love, high-performing team members work together to focus on the task at hand and get things done. But great teams require great leaders—people who can assess the situation, provide resources, and create an environment of psychological safety for their teams to thrive.

This is where servant leadership comes in. To put it mildly, prior to 2016, Softway's leaders weren't great at fostering psychological safety, offering feedback, or otherwise supporting their teams. Nasty-grams about refrigerator etiquette were the norm rather than the exception. Unsurprisingly, that harsh feedback style made its way through the organization; if the CEO saw that as acceptable behavior, then others felt empowered to behave the same way.

Once Mohammad embraced love and began working to change his own feedback style, he realized that changing himself wasn't enough to fix the feedback problem. For a culture of love to grow, every leader and role player would have to buy into a love-based communication strategy as well.

This realization led to some soul searching. How could he encourage leaders to adopt our Six Pillars of Love in how they managed, coached, and gave feedback to their teams? Moreover, if the goal of building high-functioning teams was to encourage autonomy, what did the leader's role even look like? Here is how we see the leader's role in a high-functioning team:

- **Create the vision and goals.** Do you have a vision for what the team or the organization is doing? Are everyone's goals aligned with that vision? Meaningful progress cannot happen without it.
- **Establish the identity and mission.** The leader creates the identity and mission of each team. The team should understand why it exists.
- **Set expectations and facilitate conversations.** How will the team communicate? Does everyone understand the expectations? Leaders facilitate the team's conversations around working agreements and norms to create alignment in the group.
- **Focus on results.** Naturally, to have a high-performing team, you must perform. This doesn't just mean throwing time at a problem. Eighty hours spent with no clear results are eighty hours wasted. Help team members look practically at what they're trying to accomplish and how they can maximize their time and resources.

◆ **Generate psychological safety.** Have you ever had so much fun working on a project that coming to work and throwing down with your teammates was the best part of your day? Love-focused leaders help make work feel exciting and meaningful.

These are essential behaviors of any leader on a high-performing team. However, let's be clear: Leaders cannot change a team's culture on their own. Each individual team member must also embrace these behaviors for a culture of love to thrive. Everyone is responsible for both their team's and their organization's culture. Every team member is responsible for their own transformation.

Doing Your Part

As we get ready to push on to the next chapter, we return to a question we posed earlier in the book: How do you change the culture of an organization with hundreds, thousands, maybe even tens of thousands of employees?

The answer: You don't.

Instead, you change your own behaviors first. Your behavior is your responsibility. Whether you're behaving or misbehaving—whether you're building or destroying a culture of love—that behavior is contagious.

At some point in your career, you've probably had to work with someone with a prickly personality, someone with a fixed mindset who saw every new challenge as an insurmountable problem. How did you receive this person? Did the apathy and disassociation kick in as you sought ways to work around this person? Or did you examine your own behaviors with that teammate and look for a better way forward?

None of us should be defined by our own worst traits and tendencies. Each of us can learn how to behave actively and collaboratively as part of a high-functioning team. In our experience, that's how the best teams work. Sometimes we just need someone to show us the way, to invite us in, and to remind us that our contributions matter too. In Chapter 12, we' explore all the many ways to do just that.

Questions for "We Are Better Together"

◆ Out of the five traits of high-performing teams, which trait(s) does your team excel at?

◆ Out of those same traits, which areas does your team struggle with currently? Why?

◆ What is the secret to effective teams?

◆ Feedback is a gift. When was the last time you shared the gift of feedback with someone? How did you package it?

◆ What does it look like when feedback does not flow freely?

◆ Share a story of a time you've either given or received bad feedback.

◆ Share a story of a time you've either given or received good feedback.

◆ How have you experienced leaders creating psychological safety for others?

◆ How have you experienced leaders destroying psychological safety for others?

◆ Share a story about how you've helped to foster psychological safety for your peers or team members.

◆ Thinking practically, what can you start doing immediately to incorporate psychological safety into the way you lead?

◆ After reading this chapter, are you skeptical about creating high-performing teams in the workplace? If so, share those thoughts with the group.

◆ What were some of your biggest takeaways or *ah-ha* moments from this chapter?

◆ Share a moment of self-awareness about your leadership after reading this chapter.

◆ What, if anything, will you change or adjust about how you lead or behave based on what you've read?

Note

1. Faaiza Rashid, Amy C. Edmondson, and Herman B. Leonard, "Leadership Lessons from the Chilean Mine Rescue," *Harvard Business Review* (July-August 2013). hbr.org/2013/07/leadership-lessons-from-the-chilean-mine-rescue

CHAPTER 12

HR (Humanity Required)

The Softway that Chris would come to know and love was not the Softway that greeted him.

It was late 2015. Chris was about to start his first day at the company, and he was excited. He didn't know about our rampant misbehaviors. He didn't know we had just entered a downturn. He didn't know we were a month away from laying off over a hundred team members.

Chris was surprised there was no one there to greet him as he walked through the lobby—no receptionist, no onboarding manager, no HR representative, or anything. As he stopped at a fork in the hallway, a distracted Mohammad almost ran right into him.

"Oh! You're starting today. I'd forgotten." Mohammad smiled, clearly stressed about something. "I'm sorry, I don't have any time for you, but our HR director will get you squared away."

Okay, but where was HR? Was the HR director even expecting him?

Chris continued his search through Softway's halls. Finally he found the HR director, grabbed a seat, and began filling out paperwork. Neither he nor the HR director knew what to do next. She looked at Chris. Chris looked back awkwardly. Because no one had been expecting him, the HR director didn't know where to send him next.

"Do you have any questions about Softway before you go to your desk?" she finally asked.

Chris shifted in his chair. "Um. Well. I can tell you what I know. If I'm missing anything, maybe you can fill in the gaps for me." She agreed. He talked for about ten minutes, and as he did, her eyes got wider and wider.

"Oh, wow. You know more than I do," she said after he finished. How strange.

By now Chris was getting antsy. So far, in less than two hours, the CEO had blown him off, and HR treated him with bemusement. But, since he was here, he might as well try to find his desk.

Once there, Chris glanced down at his desk to find a laptop with a sticky note attached to the top with his username and password. His username was spelled wrong, and his password didn't work. He couldn't log in. Time for another trip around the office.

"Hi, I'm told you're in charge of laptops," Chris said as he rapped on the IT guy's door. "Two things. I started today, and my name's misspelled and I can't log into the laptop."

The team member stared back at Chris. "Do you want me to change the spelling, or are you okay with keeping it?" he said, clearly hoping for the latter.

Not wanting to sound like a jerk, Chris thought up a diplomatic reply. "Yes, my email address should reflect the accurate spelling of my name. I'd hate for a client to get confused and for me to miss an email if they spelled it correctly," he said. "So, yes, please. I also need to be able to log in."

The team member took the laptop. Chris stood around—literally twiddling his thumbs—until his computer was ready and he could go back to his desk. As his new coworkers walked past the office, Chris would wave, they would wave back, and that was it. No one stopped to say hi. No one asked who he was, what he was doing (literally nothing), or whether they could help. Eventually he packed up his stuff and headed home.

Worst. First. Day. Ever. (Okay, maybe second worst. On Jeff's first day, he had to assemble his $60 desk and $29 chair by himself. But that's another story for another time.)

Chris came back the next day. And the day after that. And the day after that. And we're lucky he did. We're even luckier that after that horrible, rotten, no-good day, Chris vowed that no one at Softway would ever have a first-day experience like that again.

It's easy to look back now and laugh at how bad Chris's initial experience was, but here's the thing: First impressions matter—a lot. In fact, research shows that a person's first ninety days at a new company will determine whether they feel at home the rest of their time there.[1] How you recruit, how you hire, and how you manage and grow your talent matters.

And yet many organizations treat these processes almost as an afterthought. They outsource and automate recruiting tasks using third-party providers. They optimize for keywords rather than focus on a candidate's ability to solve problems or connect with teammates. They ignore the humanity of their candidates, intent only on confirming their bias toward a certain kind of candidate through the filters and automations they put in place.

We used to do the same thing. Thankfully, we eventually realized that our cookie-cutter checklist only produced cookie-cutter candidates. We were missing out on candidates whose life experiences might have better suited the roles we needed to fill, marginalizing their experience and wisdom in favor of an algorithm and limiting our hiring options.

In a culture of love, people are the whole point. And yet there was no humanity at all in the way we hired our people.

As we began our journey toward a culture of love, we worked to put people at the center of every step of our talent management process—from recruiting and hiring to managing and promoting. Our goals were threefold:

1. Infuse the process with humanity.
2. Identify the key traits of our candidates' personalities.
3. Ask not just whether a candidate would be good for the job but whether they'd be good for a culture of love.

In other words, the question wasn't just: Can this person do the job? It was whether we would want to be around them. Would we want to hang out with this person? Would we want to sit next to them? How would they help us solve problems differently?

Checking a box that said someone had three years of experience and a certification didn't get us what we really wanted. But maybe learning about who these people were and how we could best serve each other might. In the next sections, we'll share the story of that journey and what we learned along the way.

Hiring for Success

Have you ever received a detailed agenda and comprehensive instructions on what to expect *ahead* of an interview? Softway candidates do.

Our recruiters see themselves as advocates for our candidates. They want to give each candidate everything they need to succeed. No surprises. No mind games. No tricks of any kind. When our candidates show up to an interview, we want to empower them to represent the best versions of themselves and set the expectation that we will be doing the same. After all, any job interview is just as much for the candidate as it is for us. The more they can meet the teams they'll be working with and understand how those teams work, the more they'll be at ease on interview day.

To achieve this, we take a few different approaches. First, the day before their interview, a recruiter calls the candidate and tells them what to expect, who they'll be interviewing with, and what the interviewer is like—including their personality, their interview style, and their pet peeves. For instance, if the candidate is interviewing with Jeff, the recruiter tells them that Jeff likes to give people little puzzles to see how they solve problems. Or if the candidate is interviewing with Mohammad, the recruiter tells them that Mohammad loves punctuality—and talking about University of Houston football. Whatever information we think might help the candidate succeed, we make sure they know.

Many HR leaders are confused when we describe this step. Why put so much effort into those detailed instructions? Simple: It shows us who the candidates are. If someone can't follow directions now, they won't suddenly learn on the job. If they're arrogant to a lowly recruiter, they will also be arrogant on the job. This one step separates those who can learn and be coached from those who can't, those who will fit in with our unique culture from those who won't. This distinction in turn helps us to identify and hire candidates who might have otherwise fallen through the cracks.

Next, we take a team approach to the interviews. This is for our benefit as much as the candidates', allowing our teams to *meet* people who might eventually work with them. We approach these interviews as a series of friendly chats. Many organizations try to trip up job candidates with hardball questions, interruptions, and other challenges.

We see no use for that approach. Neither Softway nor our clients would ever treat a team member that way. Rather than trying to stress our candidates, we work to make them feel as if they belong. That way, even if we don't extend an offer, that person might consider applying to work with us in the future.

Once the interviews have concluded, the entire team gets together to learn how the interaction went. We check to see whether anyone felt marginalized or uncomfortable at any point in the conversation. (You'd be surprised how many candidates never make eye contact with a particular person.) In this way, we ensure that any new hire adds to the culture and models inclusive behaviors.

Finding the Right People

Branden hadn't had an easy life. At fifteen, he was homeless. By twenty-one, he was at the end of his rope, toiling away at a startup for months on end without getting paid. In fact, the startup was costing *him* money by running up expenses on his credit card. On top of that, he had a serious medical condition with no health insurance to treat it, and he could barely afford to eat.

We didn't know any of this about Branden when he applied for the role of designer. All we knew was that he had talent, enthusiasm, and a gentle way about him. Although the designer role wasn't a good fit for him, we liked the combination of traits he brought to the table, so we asked him to interview for the project coordinator role instead. He accepted and soared through his interviews.

Our attention paid off. Branden was so taken with us that he vowed not to apply or interview for any other jobs until he heard a *no* from Softway. He nearly fainted when we called to offer him the job.

Fast forward a couple of years later, and Branden became one of our high-performing employees. Because of his gratitude that we took a chance on him, he regularly excelled in his work, going above and beyond at every turn.

Our commitment to finding the right people gives us a competitive advantage in a challenging job market. After all, we're not the biggest company in the pond, so we must work to stand out in some other way. Softway candidates never forget how they were treated. They never forget that they were included from Day 1 and given all the tools they needed to succeed. They never forget that we've given them a chance that no one else would. In turn, they respond with incredible work, dedication, and passion.

Hiring with Love = More Diverse Teams

Don't recruit as if you're painting by numbers. Be open to different backgrounds and experiences.

In the past, we often made the mistake of hiring only people like ourselves. New recruits usually had similar levels of education, had similar skills, talked like us, and otherwise reminded us of ourselves.

This practice might have been good for the ego, but it limited our growth. Hiring people who already thought like us didn't help us innovate or create better systems and processes. It just maintained the status quo.

Once we embraced love as a recruiting strategy, our workforce began to grow more diverse. Today we have people from different ethnicities, different economic and educational backgrounds, and different parts of the world—and we've seen that diversity lead directly to innovation and growth.

You can create these results too. Consider candidates with nonstandard backgrounds for open roles. Look beyond the resume to see the real person behind it. Rather than hire only people who have been in similar positions, consider that person's ability to do the job.

A Raise on the Spot

Softway once had a rigid performance management system, particularly in our India office. We asked each employee for a personal assessment, provided a manager's assessment, used a rubric to fill in the rest, and then calculated a person's raise for the year.

It was a stressful experience for everyone, and it didn't work very well. Although we'd designed the system to be data-driven and unbiased, in practice, it just rewarded tenure and favorites.

How did this happen? Well, there were core flaws in the system:

- A team member's reviewing manager was not the same person who oversaw their work. As a result, no reviewing manager could accurately assess performance.
- Unable to produce objective evaluations, managers disengaged from salary conversations—what we call *fish market negotiations*. Rather than listen to the employee's very real objections, managers simply rewarded favorite employees and retaliated against least favorites.
- The system deprivileged actual performance. No one received feedback until their annual review, and because the evaluating manager wasn't their actual manager, that feedback was sparse and lacking context.

Our approach wasn't unusual, but it wasn't helping the talented people in our organization grow their skill sets. This in turn led to a *brain drain*: The best (and underappreciated) team members left, while the mediocre team members gamed a system that strongly rewarded tenure.

One day we came across an article about an organization that practiced what they called "spot raises." The article's argument was simple: If a person did great work, they deserved a raise—whether that was every week, every two months, or every two years. As we transitioned to a culture of love, we decided to embrace a similar system. No more stressful annual reviews that left everyone disappointed. Instead, we established new, real-time methods of evaluating and rewarding performance.

At first, some team members were suspicious of this new system and all our talk about "earning it." Then they saw it in action. The high performers, in particular, quickly found that they could influence their pay in a direct and powerful way, whether through their performance or by growing their skill sets. Just as we had said, if they did excellent work, that work was noticed and rewarded.

As an added bonus, our teams got better at giving and receiving feedback as well. Because team members saw a direct correlation to effort and reward, they became more focused on growing their skills and taking on challenges they previously wouldn't have touched. In that way, the change was a win-win: We benefited from improved performance, and team members benefited by growing their skills and bank accounts.

Promotional Equity

In organizations with diverse talent, people from nondominant groups typically are promoted more slowly than people from dominant groups. Eventually people from nondominant groups begin to feel they won't be able to realize their potential within the organization, and they leave.

Unfortunately, this pattern reinforces the notion internally that nondominant groups are not as capable. That negative bias infiltrates performance management, recruiting, onboarding, training, and development. It perpetuates itself, becoming a self-fulfilling prophecy.

In a culture of love, you're committed to realizing the potential in everyone. If you're acting on this commitment, everyone should see the opportunity to earn promotions within the organization.

Agile Talent Management

Around the time we were altering our performance management system, we also reorganized so that leaders could build real relationships with their direct reports. To do that, we built cross-functional teams oriented around a specific project or type of project where team leaders could actually *see* the work they created. These practices reflect what is known as an *Agile* methodology. (See Chapter 15 for the full story of how we went Agile.)

This shift was a welcome change, but one byproduct was that it complicated career paths. Typically, as a person builds an increasingly specialized skill set, their career trajectory moves in a straight line. In Agile teams, however, people often develop into deep generalists, with specific expertise in one area and general skills in others.

While this T-shaped skill set creates more options for both the team and team members, it also removes linear career paths. Why? Because Agile processes do away with the typical manager role. Instead, team members have two key roles: facilitator and leader. Anyone can lead an Agile team without management experience and without giving up their day-to-day work. They can also grow their skill sets: On any given project, a designer could tackle copywriting, a coder could be a project manager, and so on.

This shift to Agile didn't feel natural at first, and many team members pushed back. But once people saw the flexibility Agile gave them in their work, they saw how effective this approach was in breaking down silos and removing barriers to getting work done. No longer did team members have to wait for the "expert" to become available in order to do a basic thing. Instead, anyone could step in to fill needs as they identify them—and therefore tackle any challenge they're given. The more psychological safety they build and the better their teamwork, the more they're able to accomplish.

This was all good news for Softway, but what about our team members? By privileging a culture of deep generalists, weren't we pushing people off their career paths? In our experience, this hasn't been the case. In fact, we've found the opposite to be true. A graphic designer who steps in to do a little copywriting is still a graphic designer and still on that career path. But now they've expanded their skill set and become more competent in their job in ways by developing complementary skills. Offering our team members new ways of working and new approaches to problem-solving provides them with *more* options for their careers, not fewer.

Every Day Should Feel Like Friday

Love as a Business Strategy forced us to rethink every aspect of our recruiting, hiring, onboarding, and management processes. We've come a long way since Chris's worst first day ever.

These days we start new team members on Fridays. (Unless it's one of the every other Fridays that we have off.) Back in the day before we went mixed hybrid (a blend of in-person and remote depending on the need), we would greet new hires personally when they arrived and show them to their desk—where a basket of hand-picked treats awaited (another perk of getting to know our new hires during the interview process). Now that we're mixed hybrid, we believe it's even more important to get the new hires' first day right: Each new hire receives a swag pack (with said hand-picked treats) along with their work computer and a personalized virtual greeting.

From there, whether in-person or remote, we dedicate the first few *weeks* to building relationships. Every new hire has a jam-packed agenda full of welcome meetings. Through the course of these meetings, they'll meet their new team, their supervisor, and all sorts of other folks—even people they won't regularly work with. Afterward, we introduce them to the company during our end-of-the-week standup meeting, where we like to keep it loose and fun. Then we either send them out for lunch with their team or send them an UberEats or Door Dash gift card so they can enjoy their first team meal on us. No one eats alone on their first day! For the rest of the day, we set up meetings across the organization. New hires quickly get up to speed with their closest contacts, and then they get the chance to meet people outside of their team.

And then they're done—and ready to enjoy the weekend.

In our view, this is the best possible introduction. After all, there's nothing like getting two days off for one day of work!

Making our team members feel welcome and included from the moment they set foot in the door isn't just good for morale. It's good for business. In fact, as we'll see in the next chapter, it's the key driver of our business outcomes.

Questions for "HR (Humanity Required)"

- ◆ Share some ways that HR can champion Love as a Business Strategy in your organization.
- ◆ Considering Chris's terrible, horrible, no-good, very-bad first-day experience, what are first days like at your workplace?
- ◆ How could empathy factor into the onboarding experience?

- First impressions matter. How are you creating the right (or wrong) impression for those you're looking to hire?
- Are you setting up candidates to succeed? How can you create a more empowering experience for potential hires?
- How can you weave more humanity into the way you recruit?
- Considering Branden and his past, how can you be more inclusive with your approach to recruiting potential employees?
- How can you help every day feel like Friday?
- Thinking practically, what can you start doing immediately to incorporate some of these ideas into your HR practices or department?
- After reading this chapter, are you skeptical about the way Softway recruits and onboards new team members? If so, share those thoughts with the group.
- What were some of your biggest takeaways or *ah-ha* moments from this chapter?
- Share a moment of self-awareness about your leadership after reading this chapter.
- What, if anything, will you change or adjust about how you lead or behave based on what you've read?

Note

1. Arlene S. Hirsch, "Don't Underestimate the Importance of Good Onboarding," *SHRM*, August 10, 2017. www.shrm.org/topics-tools/news/talent-acquisition/dont-underestimate-importance-good-onboarding

CHAPTER 13

Systems—People, Process, and Technology

The old Softway suffered from systemic mistrust. Our choices regarding our people, processes, and technology all reflected that.

We thought we were doing the right things to improve our business. In reality, we were creating harm and holding our team back. Worse, our choices didn't work. All we did was create more inefficiency in the name of efficiency.

Nowhere was this more evident than in our choice to install a biometric tracking system in our Bengaluru, India, office. We told our team members that this system was purely for security and confidentiality.

That was only partially true. We also used it to track the comings and goings of our team members and punish them for being tardy. If we did not have a team member's fingerprint in our system by eleven in the morning, we docked their pay and instructed HR to call them into work. When the team member finally did show up, they would not be paid for the day until HR formally excused them.

Not only was this system both dehumanizing and marginalizing (notice how we didn't install the same system in our Houston, Texas, office), but it was also inefficient. As we learned from Sunil, one of the HR employees tasked with tracking down those tardy team members (see Chapter 5), this took a lot of work—literally the entire morning.

This massive time expenditure was no good. We wanted HR to spend their time recruiting, screening, hiring, and developing new employees. That's what they wanted to do too, but because we'd also made them our de facto truant officers, they couldn't. As a result, they constantly took flak from their direct reports, who didn't understand why so little progress was being made. Sunil and his teammates understood the problem all too well, but they were powerless to change it.

Of course, they weren't the only ones trapped in this corporate hell. Our tracking system created problems everywhere. For instance, if someone went on an approved vacation for four or five days without formally submitting a request, the system would mark them as absent and dock their pay—all without any warning. Imagine opening a paycheck at the end of the month only to find out it was just a *third* of what you were expecting!

You wouldn't feel very good. None of our employees in Bengaluru felt very good either. Eventually they made their displeasure known. *More* team members began showing up late to work, if at all. They didn't appreciate HR behaving like overzealous parents, they didn't appreciate the phone calls at all hours of the day, and they especially didn't appreciate their pay being docked. The more we dehumanized them, the less they wanted to work.

Funny how that happens, isn't it?

At the risk of stating the obvious, docking employees' pay without telling them—and then making them jump through a series of bureaucratic hoops to correct the issue—is antithetical to a culture of love. To be clear, the problem wasn't with the biometric scanners. The tool itself is rarely the problem. The problem was the rampant mistrust baked into the very fabric of our culture. We lacked the trust and empathy to deploy that tool with compassion, choosing instead to promote a culture of fear. As a result of our misbehaviors, many of our Bengaluru employees struggled to make ends meet.

Here again, Softway was no different from many companies. Leaders often turn to processes and technology in the name of efficiency and innovation. They may mean well by these initiatives, but approached from the mistrusting mindset, the results are often the opposite of what they expected.

Now we know better. These days, no matter how technical the process or mundane the system, we approach every policy decision through a lens of love. We're constantly asking how our decisions and interactions impact others. If our systems don't reflect our desire to put people first, then our claim to have a culture of love would be meaningless.

Take those biometric scanners, for example. It may surprise you to learn we still have them—but we don't use them much. These days we use them only for after-hours security so that our team members feel safer when they're at the office working late. It's still the same system, but our intentions have changed, and so has the impact. Instead of using these scanners to spy on our employees, we use them to reflect our investment in their physical and mental well-being. Seeing our commitment to putting people first, not only do our team members trust us again, but productivity has skyrocketed.

In this chapter we're going to talk about how to view your systems in a culture of love. To do that, instead of looking at each area of your organization one by one (e.g., operations, sales, marketing, etc.), we're going to zoom in on the common thread running through every part of your organization: people. When you focus on how you can best support your people, all decisions on processes and tools will flow naturally from there.

Process Isn't the Way Out

When faced with challenges, most organizations try to solve them by adding in more processes. For years, we were no different. And yet, for every new bit of process we added, our results didn't change. Sales didn't improve. Engagement didn't increase. If anything, our results got worse.

Still, we didn't learn. Whatever the specifics, whatever the department, the next time a problem came up, our approach to the problem was the same: Look at the process again, add more steps, and demand that our teams follow each one to the letter.

We wanted to build a more efficient business. Instead, we built a pressure cooker. Team members fell farther and farther behind, we put up more barriers to execution, and team members fell even farther behind, and so on. Wash, rinse, repeat.

For years, we were convinced that the failure wasn't with us but with our employes. We couldn't see all the ways we were setting our team members up for failure. We couldn't see how our mistrust in one area caused a chain reaction of problems in others. We couldn't see how our relentless focus on process and tech was failing all the living, breathing people who did the work. And because we couldn't see these things, we had no empathy for our team members when they struggled.

Talk about disempowering. How can you take ownership of your work or take pride in what you do if your every move is scrutinized, cataloged, and reported? What incentive do you have to innovate when you live in fear of showing up late? How will you offer solutions when every time you try to raise a red flag, you're excluded from the conversation?

To answer those questions in order: You can't, you don't, and you won't.

Such was the state of Softway in 2015. Unforgiveness and mistrust were everywhere. Team members didn't practice vulnerability; they practiced self-preservation. Often this meant playing the blame game. Take the story of the biometric scanners, for example:

◆ Management in HR blamed their teams for missing their quotas.
◆ HR teams blamed all the tardy employees for distracting them from recruiting.
◆ Tardy employees blamed the weather, their dogs, or anything else so they wouldn't have to admit that they were miserable at their job—but also terrified of losing it.

The system we had built was fundamentally broken. Eventually something had to give—and it did, in the form of our 2015 downturn.

Afterward, we finally began to understand that when things went wrong, it wasn't because of a tech problem or a process problem. It was because of a *people* problem. If your people don't feel empowered to trust each other and do their jobs, you're going to have issues—and no one will care enough to fix them. In such an environment, layering more processes on top of the dysfunction will only make it worse.

Problems aren't fixed through process and technology. They're fixed through culture, behavior, and team dynamics.

Inspecting and Introspecting Your Systems

When confronted with a system that doesn't work as it should, often we look for ways to tweak, add to, or otherwise modify the system. Rarely do we ask whether the system itself is critically flawed. As you examine your own systems, ask:

- When you designed your processes or adopted new technologies, what outcomes did you envision? What outcomes did you actually produce?
- How might your processes and tech adoption be hindering your people—and therefore your organization—from fully thriving?
- How would your systems change if you designed them around the Six Pillars of Love? What kinds of attitudes, mindsets, and behaviors would those systems promote? How would your processes and tech adoption change?
- How can you integrate your values into the day-to-day realities of your organizational decisions?

Don't Get Trapped

Since its beginning, Softway has been in the business of solving problems for other organizations. But it wasn't until we began to introspect and understand our own problems that we were able to fully deliver on that promise to our customers. To fully deliver, we had to learn to build our systems around our people, not on processes or technology.

Slowly things began to change. Once our team members felt psychologically safe that they could speak and give feedback freely, we began to innovate in ways we never had before. Further, these changes could be felt throughout the organization—from our sales team to our project managers, from our creatives to our technologists. Because our systems were all designed to reflect our investment in our teams, our teams invested in us.

It took time to turn the ship, but eventually we saw the results that we had hoped for. In 2015 we had low average contract values, little repeat business, and process issues that put our project managers and fulfillment team into perpetual firefighting mode. By 2019 our average client value had quintupled, we were consistently attracting repeat business, and we had repositioned ourselves to partner with clients and create lasting change rather than put out fires for them. The transformation was astonishing.

Again, this transformation wasn't about a process or a tech change—though those happened too. Instead, we looked at the dysfunction, unforgiveness, and mistrust inherent in our system and made a *people* change. Remember: All processes are made by people. Most processes are performed by people. Don't forget the fundamental humanity that drives them.

Like many organizations, it was easy for us to fall into the process trap. But eventually we found ourselves struggling to find our way through a labyrinth of our own making. We didn't *want* to be trapped in this labyrinth, of course. We wanted simplicity. We wanted efficiency. We wanted results. We truly believed that systems changes like the biometric scanners would help serve those ends.

Of course, that's not what happened. Because we didn't consider our people whenever a systems change was considered, we caused our people legitimate harm instead. When we docked employees' pay without warning, we made it harder for team members to provide for their families. When we forced HR to police the entire workforce, we prevented them from achieving their recruiting goals. When we based our decisions on mistrust and unforgiveness, we prevented ourselves from inspiring our teams and driving innovation within the company.

Whatever transformation you are trying to bring to your own organization, never forget that processes and technology merely reflect the decisions made by people. Do those people have the right mindset and behaviors? Are they supporting and empowering team members or putting them in a pressure cooker of mistrust? To drive the outcomes that will take your organization to the next level, you must start with people.

Putting People First

To learn more about how Softway found a balance between process and behaviors, visit www.LoveAsAStrategy.com/resources.

Questions for "Systems—People, Process, Tech"

- ◆ Why do leaders allow systems, policies, and processes to dictate behavior?
- ◆ What systems or policies do you have in place that erode trust between team members and leadership? Why are they still in use?
- ◆ When the Six Pillars of Love aren't considered, what types of policies or processes are put in place?
- ◆ Thinking practically, can you name current processes or policies that were most likely a result of unforgiveness toward people in your organization? If so, what were they?
- ◆ Why do leaders rush to create more processes to solve problems instead of focusing on culture, behavior, and team dynamics?
- ◆ How are your current systems, processes, and policies impacting psychological safety of your team?
- ◆ You've got a magic wand. Congrats! What policies and processes have you erased from existence, and how does your culture improve as a result?
- ◆ Considering the Six Pillars of Love, how could those behaviors begin to transform your strategic layer of people, process, and tools?
- ◆ Thinking practically, what can you start doing immediately to transform your approach to implementing systems, policies, and processes?

- What were some of your biggest takeaways or *ah-ha* moments from this chapter?
- Share a moment of self-awareness about your leadership after reading this chapter.
- What, if anything, will you change or adjust about how you lead or behave based on what you've read?

CHAPTER 14

Lovin' Those Business Outcomes

Between late 2015 and the end of 2016, Softway was on the verge of bankruptcy.

Our EBITDA stood at negative 15 percent. We were hemorrhaging cash and staring down huge seven-figure losses. We owed everyone money—the banks, the credit card companies, our landlords, some loan shark named "Cousin Lou," you name it.

We had tried to be proactive by laying off a third of our workforce, but the payroll relief was already too little, too late. To keep the company afloat, Mohammad liquidated all his assets and even borrowed money from his family.

It was rough going there for a while, but we got through it. Barely.

That's why, when people ask us if a culture of love *really* improves outcomes, we point to ourselves as Example Numero Uno. Just three years after we almost collapsed, Softway was growing, profitable, and debt-free. Between 2016 to 2019, we saw a remarkable turnaround in our outcomes:

- ◆ **Revenue:** Increased by 300 percent
- ◆ **EBITDA or profit:** Increased by 43 percent, bringing it to a positive 28 percent
- ◆ **Average project size:** Increased by 750 percent, putting our contracts into six and seven figures
- ◆ **Average account size:** Increased by 985 percent

+ **Client retention rate:** Grew from 60 to 90 percent
+ **Revenue per employee:** Increased by 269 percent
+ **Average employee tenure:** Our team members were not only staying longer, but they were also happier.
+ **Attrition (combined for India and the United States):**
  - 2016: over 30 percent
  - 2019: 12 percent
  - 2023: Under 5 percent
+ **Glassdoor rating:**
  - 2016: 2.9
  - 2020 (when we wrote this book): above 4.0
  - 2024: 4.2

A note on attrition: For comparison, the technology industry in the United States averages 13 percent attrition, while in India it averages 28 percent. Our attrition was lower than our peers' in both countries.

That said, here's what the numbers don't capture. For years before our downturn, Softway looked like a success on paper. But our unforgiveness, misbehaviors, and structural greed caught up to us. The issues became so systemic that we stopped making money.

Through our transformation, we learned a valuable lesson. If you're only looking at your bottom line and watching your accounts grow every quarter, you might think you're okay. But ask yourself: What problems are sitting just below the surface? What are the numbers hiding that you're not looking for?

For over a decade, we didn't take these kinds of questions seriously. We looked at our issues, shrugged, and said, "That's just the way we're built." Our denial was almost our undoing.

You have the opportunity to learn from our mistakes and address your own systemic misbehaviors. What opportunities could you embrace if your culture changed for the better? What could your people do if they were empowered and supported?

When you commit to supporting your people and building a culture of love around them, your outcomes will improve in almost every way. In this chapter we show you the people-centric outcomes that we focus on to drive bottom-line growth.

What Are Your Target Outcomes?

Over the past several years, we've worked with a vast array of organizations—including school systems, governments, and nonprofits—that may not focus on EBITDA as one of their target outcomes. Here are some of the outcomes these organizations defined to help them measure the success of their culture of love:

- **Education:** Student and faculty success, equity and access, financial stability, parent and guardian engagement.
- **Nonprofits:** Donor support, mission impact, and sustainable funding.
- **Governments:** Cost reduction, operational efficiency, quality, reliability, workforce development, and policy implementation.
- **Healthcare:** Patient safety, quality of care, clinician engagement, and operational efficiency.

As you can see, your target outcomes will fluctuate depending on your goals and the nature of your work. But one thing we've learned: Our framework helps maximize *any* outcome, regardless of business type.

People Drive Outcomes

Softway works in technology. We like data. A lot.

Data gives you the background you need to be confident about your decisions and the direction in which you're moving. That said, data isn't the end-all, be-all. Numbers alone will never tell you the whole story. In fact, we've come to see them as lagging indicators of success rather than leading indicators. After all, behind every number, behind every metric, are the people who create them.

People are the biggest driver of sustainability. Period. If you want to move the needle, then create favorable conditions for your people to drive the outcomes you're looking for. For instance:

- ◆ If you want your team to feel sharp and ready to work on an international trip, bump their flights up to business class.
- ◆ If you want high-performing teams, teach your teams how to build trusting relationships.
- ◆ If you want repeat business, serve your teams so they can serve your customer.

Do these investments come with a cost? Yes, but almost every time, the cost is worth it. Take care of your people, and they will take care of your organization. In the next sections, we'll show you how to set this process in motion.

Winning the Talent War with Love

There always has been and always will be a war for talent. Every company is looking for the best and brightest available on the market. Our culture of love gives us a competitive edge in the marketplace. As a result, we have an easier time identifying, attracting, and recruiting people to our organization.

This is a great position to be in—and a far cry from a few years earlier, when we'd take out job ads and spend endless days and dollars headhunting on LinkedIn. These days we often fill positions on referrals alone. Our team members love sending good candidates our way. All we have to do is announce our open positions and describe what we're looking for. Before we know it, six team members have suggested friends who are eager for the opportunity to come work with us.

When we do have to go out and recruit good candidates, Love as a Business Strategy has made that process easier too. Previously potential candidates often wouldn't return our calls. Today they're intrigued by our culture and happy to respond. From there, it's just a matter of connecting on a call and telling them what we're all about so we can kick off the interview process.

Through these efforts, we've gained access to much better talent. Some of these candidates even turn down larger offers at better-known organizations for the opportunity to work at Softway. They're impressed by our recruiting experience, they like how we conduct ourselves during the interview process, and they're encouraged by our reviews on sites like Glassdoor. As a midmarket challenger with nowhere near the name recognition of the bigger fish like Google, we can punch well above our weight as a result of our culture of love.

RETAINING THE RIGHT PEOPLE

As a Black man, Chris has worked in many companies where his opportunities either were limited or required him to become someone he was not. At Softway, Chris is empowered to be exactly who he is without worrying about the political games he would have to play elsewhere.

Like many of our other team members, Chris has thrived in this environment. And, also like many of our other team members, Chris is often approached by other companies attempting to poach him.

Every time Chris receives a message from another organization, he forwards it to Mohammad, along with a single sentence: "I'm not going anywhere."

Mohammad loves getting those emails.

So, what's the lesson here? Once you've attracted good people, you need to retain them. Two reasons why:

1. Better employee retention means a healthier bottom line.
2. When a valued team member walks out the door, they take both their talent and deep knowledge of your organization with them.

The talent you can replace. The knowledge, however, is a little trickier. According to some estimates, up to 60 percent of a person's role is undocumented—even in an organization that's great at documenting. This fact presents a compounding problem: The longer a person's tenure, the more knowledge they've accumulated, and the harder it is to replicate that knowledge and skill set. A new hire will get there eventually, but in the meantime, your organization pays the price in both time and opportunity costs.

Many of these costs don't appear as an entry in the balance sheet. They're hidden within so many other entries that leaders often don't see them. But the impact is real…and expensive. Every time you stop a high-performing person from walking out the door, you're keeping a pile of cash in the company's coffers.

Softway's improved attrition rate isn't just good for business. It's also a source of pride. When people like Chris turn down opportunities elsewhere, it demonstrates that our commitment to people is working.

SAYING GOOD-BYE TO THE WRONG PEOPLE

Although losing the right person is costly, so is keeping the wrong person. Even in a culture of love (we would argue *especially* in a culture of love), you have to know when to let team members go.

In many organizations, people who aren't contributing, resilient, or behaving well often feel safe enough to ignore company policy. They know that finding a job elsewhere would be difficult, so they do just enough to get by. Meanwhile, each misbehavior poisons the culture a little more, alienating the best, most productive team members—who eventually leave to do their best work somewhere else. We've lost several rock stars we still miss due to other team members' misbehaviors, and we regret not stepping in to change the culture surrounding those star performers early and decisively.

We've also struggled with problematic leaders. For instance, not everyone was on board with our shift to a culture of love. They rejected the chance to become servant leaders, our focus on people, and our emphasis on personal growth, inclusion, and development. Further, they did not see themselves clearly, they rejected feedback, and they rejected invitations to work on their behavior.

These leaders' attitudes affected not only the health of our culture but also the performance of their teams. Following the old, command-and-control style of leadership Softway used to practice, these leaders micromanaged and dictated responsibilities to their teams. They set rigid expectations, demanding that each worker stay till five on the dot every day, even if those workers were finished at four and had no more meaningful work left to do. With no agency and no respect, these workers adopted a fixed mindset and disengaged. As a result, their work suffered.

Elsewhere, the teams whose leaders had embraced servant leadership were excelling. Members of these teams worked autonomously to produce innovative, creative solutions our customers loved. Seeing these stunning results, we were confident that we were onto something with our new direction as a company.

Unfortunately, because we hadn't shifted uniformly across the organization, we were still delivering inconsistent results at best. During this period, it was like a tale of two companies. Not only did our customers pay a price for our inconsistency, but so did the rest of our organization. Members of our high-performing teams in particular began to take notice. Why was it okay for certain teams to skirt expectations when everyone else was expected to uphold a higher standard?

It wasn't, and we knew it. We had been slow to recognize the problem, but now that it had our attention, we knew that we could not let these misbehaviors continue. Approaching the problem from a growth mindset, first we tried to work with these problematic leaders. They refused, and we exited them from the company. It was the right choice, but it took too long to get there. In the time we spent deciding what to do, those toxic leaders inflicted a lot of damage.

In a culture of love, we want everyone to be successful. We want to see the best for people, and we want them to grow. We are very open to criticism and very tolerant of people who have problems with the executive leadership team. After all, as we said in Chapter 1, love is speaking truth to power. That said, the moment a team member starts hurting others who are not their direct reports or part of the executive leadership team, we become far less tolerant. Such behavior is fundamentally antithetical to a culture of love. If that person is unwilling to introspect on their misbehaviors and make a change, then our only choice is to exit them before they drive away other team members we trust and value.

We cannot allow people to abuse love.

We cannot allow people—or *culture vultures*, as we lovingly call them—to take from the culture of love but not give back.

We cannot love someone so much that we allow them to harm others.

Having tough conversations is hard, but we cannot grow a culture of love without also telling the truth. If someone is not willing to follow the values that we live by, then they can't stay.

That being said, all people deserve to be treated with dignity and respect. We never want to go back to the dehumanizing way we laid off our employees in 2015. When it's clear we need to exit someone, we treat them like a human. We give them a chance, we show them what's required, and we make sure that they understand that it's their choice whether they stay or go.

CREATING FUTURE LEADERS

Project management is a tricky role to hire for. Prior to 2016, it was like rolling the dice; we didn't know who would succeed and who would fail.

Relying on PMP certification didn't work. Our projects and our clients are too varied, and every project has its own unique set of challenges. A single project manager might have to deal with moving parts from creative to technology, strategy to user experience, and everything in between. With so much variability in both the performance of the role and expected outcomes, we found it next to impossible to predict success in hiring.

As we grew into a people-focused organization, we began to see the role of project manager much differently. We didn't need certification and experience. We needed mini-CEOs—creative, autonomous thinkers who could treat each project as if it was their own little individual business. The best PMs ensure that their team innovates and delivers quality work. They understand every aspect of the business and work to keep the project profitable. They negotiate and facilitate work between different members of different teams both within Softway and within the client organization—all while keeping everyone happy and delivering the project on time.

PMs, then, are the embodiment of servant leadership. They schedule meetings, order food, remove roadblocks, and otherwise grease the wheels of success. More than anything, they are resilient, adaptive, and able to work outside of the box. By prioritizing these traits in our hires—and then by trusting and empowering them from Day 1—we have not only solidified the role, but we have become far better at executing as a company.

As an added bonus, we have also become better at incubating leaders from within. Our PMs regularly grow into other leadership positions. And because the role draws talent from a variety of backgrounds, it has also made our organizational leadership more diverse—especially in terms of gender parity.

When you change the way you hire, provide opportunities for training, and offer chances to work on challenging projects, you change the skill sets in your organization. You enable people to take risks, grow, learn, and, yes, even fail. When they do those things consistently, they'll earn promotions faster.

As you're hiring, look carefully at people from different backgrounds. Look beyond your backyard too. Our best PMs come from all over the globe. Pay particular attention to people who have service experience. Those people will be poised to adapt and grow into servant leaders.

Finally, put your people in situations where they can be challenged and take risks, and entrust them with responsibility—and give them an environment where they can succeed. People tend to grow beyond the role they're given when you allow them to do so. When someone is capable of thinking broadly and finding solutions for the organization and the customers, that person is ready to lead, regardless of the time they've spent in their role. In our experience, that promotion to leadership could happen in two years or less.

Business Sustainability

Companies often think only about short-term gain, focusing solely on revenue and shareholder returns. But product cycles are quick. Whatever you sell today could be obsolete in a year. Further, short-term thinking tends to commodify your greatest resource: people. If you're willing to put revenue ahead of your people so you can profit today, why would you be expected to do anything different tomorrow?

Resilient organizations with the right people displaying the right attitudes and right behaviors will find the new products that need to be created. They will adjust to new market conditions. They will stay ahead of the curve and embrace new ideas. They will create long-term possibilities without sacrificing short-term revenue.

The most successful organizations understand this. The less successful ones don't. Just look at Blockbuster. A long time ago, in a galaxy far, far away, Blockbuster had a thriving brick-and-mortar movie rental business. The company saw a business opportunity with streaming content long before Netflix—in fact, it had an opportunity to purchase Netflix when the company was still in its infancy—but it never acted on these insights. Why? Because Blockbuster saw the idea of streaming content as a threat to its existing business model.

Suffice it to say, inaction bankrupted the organization. By the time it debuted its streaming service, Netflix already dominated the market. Blockbuster could not compete. Now, as of this writing, only one Blockbuster store remains, while Netflix is a flourishing international brand with hundreds of millions of customers.

One of the most important roles culture can play is in making a business sustainable. The old way is costly, rigid, and slow. A culture of love is resilient, adaptable, and innovative, propelling both profit and long-term outcomes. In the next sections, we'll explore how.

THE IMPORTANCE OF RESILIENCE

No one knows the future. But you can be certain that calamity and catastrophe will come for your organization eventually. How your organization responds when disaster strikes has everything to do with the culture you have built. That's why resilience is so important. A culture that can respond quickly to change will survive the worst anyone can throw at it.

When we wrote the first edition of this book in late 2020 and early 2021, we watched as some organizations fell to the economic uncertainty created by the COVID-19 crisis while others thrived. Perhaps no industry was hit harder than the airline industry. United Airlines, American Airlines, and Delta all furloughed thousands of employees—eventually laying many of those employees off. Southwest Airlines, however, remained relatively successful.

What did Southwest do differently? It doubled down on its strengths—servant leadership and love. Rather than furlough or lay anyone off, Southwest temporarily reduced employee salaries instead. Knowing that this was a big ask, the CEO took the lead, announcing that he would take no salary whatsoever in 2020 and 2021.

It worked. Because it avoided making any big, drastic decisions that would be difficult to reverse, Southwest recovered quickly when the world slowly lurched back to life in late 2021 and began traveling again. It's not easy keeping your cool under pressure like that—especially when that pressure is an era-defining pandemic. However, Southwest's resilient culture proved more than capable of rolling with the punches.

As the late CEO of Oracle, Mark Hurd, once said, "Any idiot can cut costs. That's easy. The true measure of a leader is whether you can find revenue." When the COVID-19 pandemic hit us, we took these words to heart. Sure, we found cost savings where we could. But, like Southwest, we weren't going to cut our people to do it. Not this time.

Instead, we put our energy into rethinking how our teams would work remotely. Doing this proved a greater challenge than we had anticipated. Although our team members in America generally had internet access and could shift to remote work with relative ease, many of our team members in India did not have that luxury. As lockdowns began, many returned to their hometowns to shelter in place. In these rural areas, internet connectivity was spotty at best. Through trial and error—and a lot of patience—we found a way to make it work.

Of course, securing internet access for our Indian employees wasn't our biggest challenge. The pandemic also upended our entire business model. As a Houston-based organization, a large percentage of our clientele comes from the oil and gas industry—an industry that was already in the midst of a downturn *before* the pandemic. When the pandemic hit, these organizations began canceling our contracts en masse. Suddenly not only did we have to deal with the economic uncertainty of an international health crisis, but we also had to rethink how we served our clients…and who our clients were. To survive, we decided to transition our business from a service-based model to a product-based model—all from scratch.

Over the next several months, it was all hands on deck. Team members put in extra hours, learned new skills, and supported each other in service of the organization's shared goal. Despite their sacrifice in terms of time and energy, our teams embraced the challenge with confidence and poise. As a result, we lived to fight another day.

Without resilience, that pivot never would have happened. But it wasn't the work that we put in during the pandemic that got us through—it was the work we put in to build a culture of love for years beforehand.

Resilience can't be bought off a shelf. It must be incubated and grown over time. From the very first moment we pivoted to a culture of love, we were positioning our company to weather the unprecedented storm that was 2020.

UNLOCK INNOVATION

Innovation is the ability to create new processes, products, technologies, policies, and tools—anything that gets the organization to a new level. Innovation creates new ways of coming together, of resilience, and of rising to the market's needs. You can achieve innovation only when people are comfortable speaking up, taking risks, and letting their ideas shine.

Many companies turned the COVID crisis into innovation and opportunity. A car manufacturer transformed an assembly line to make ventilators within days. Doing so required the company to dismantle the old way and make room for the new. Fortunately, its culture was up to the task.

Innovative organizations are:

- ◆ Open to new ideas and willing to abandon the old ways of working.
- ◆ Committed to reaching the outcome by any path.
- ◆ Committed to serving their business, people, and customers however they can.

The culture of love naturally leads to these mindsets and practices. When teams prioritize inclusion, empowerment, and autonomy, they foster an environment where team members can adapt, change, and otherwise demonstrate resiliency. Not every innovation needs to be a game-changer, but sometimes the smallest moments of change can spark a change that no one could have imagined.

CREATE BELONGING

Belonging can be a difficult concept for leaders to grasp: You can't see it as data on a dashboard, and no one is ever quite sure what it means.

Here's what it means to us. In early 2020, a large portion of our company took temporary pay cuts to weather the economic downturn that resulted from the COVID-19 pandemic. Some on our executive leadership team took cuts as high as 30 percent.

One of our employees who took the pay cut, Maggie, didn't have to. As she told us later, she had offers to make more money elsewhere. But she didn't want to. In the five jobs she'd had up to that point in her career, she had never felt so respected and loved as she did in her job at Softway. In short, she felt like she belonged. (And we felt the same way.)

Belonging is the crucial ingredient to organizational and team unity. Once you feel like you belong somewhere, you will fight for it, protect it, defend it, maybe even paint your body in the team colors. If that means a temporary pay cut, then so be it.

Of course, belonging isn't all about sacrifice. It's also about feeling free to explore, emote, and connect. Everyone has each other's backs because everyone knows their success is intertwined. Since the first edition of this book came out, Maggie has left our company, but we will always consider her a part of the team (and we hope she feels the same way).

This feeling of belonging is rare in many modern organizations, especially among younger generations and diverse talent. It's not that this incoming workforce doesn't want to belong to something bigger than themselves. It's that they've never been invited to do so. That's too bad. We've found that if you can unlock this feeling of belonging in your team members, you will be rewarded not only with higher retention but with committed, dedicated daily efforts.

These results are indicators of the ultimate outcome: not merely feeling like you belong but actually belonging. When team members know they belong to an organization, they are empowered to act as leaders and double down on strengthening the culture—triggering what we call a *legacy of belonging*.

When new team members come into the fold at Softway, they are inspired by all the love, passion, and dedication around them—accelerating their own buy-in and participation in the culture. As leaders, we're amazed at how welcome new team members are made to feel, at how quickly they buy into the culture around them, and at how far we've come as an organization to get here. For those of us who were around for Softway's darkest day, this is a special feeling indeed.

HOW BAD DO YOU WANT IT?

A few years ago, we initiated a round of customer interviews to build empathy and receive feedback. They told us we were not the cheapest, but that we did good work and they had a good time working with us. Every customer agreed that working with our team meant spending time with good humans.

So many companies engage in a race to the bottom for the cheapest product. They don't care about people quality, and as a result they don't care about quality either.

When you operate in this way, not only are you leaving money on the table, but you are also creating an image of your organization that will permeate the market. Customers know if your team is miserable. They can sense it in every interaction, from how they're being taken care of to the quality of the service, and everything in between.

We've worked with many consultants from large firms. When we go out for social events, they tell us they wish they had what we have. They don't feel supported by their companies. They aren't empowered to find solutions without seeking guidance from a senior partner. This burdensome chain of command eliminates a consultant's agency, reduces their ability to connect and empathize with their clients, and squashes opportunities to pivot in real time to customer needs.

As we share in Chapter 15, when you build an organization around people, your customers will notice. They will be drawn to you. We've had great opportunities come to Softway simply because people like working with us.

Ultimately, that's what you get when you have a culture of love: People just want to be around you. But again, achieving this kind of culture isn't easy. Some people need more convincing before they sign on, while others want nothing to do with it. That's why, in Chapter 16, we're going to take a good, long look at what it takes to bring (and manage) lasting change within your organization.

Questions for "Lovin' Those Business Outcomes"

- What are some ways you can link behaviors to your bottom line?
- People drive outcomes. What are some ways that focusing on people will help create better business results?
- How are you measuring success in the talent wars?
- Share a story about the work you've done to retain talent within your organization.
- What are the impacts of keeping on board team members whom you know are hindering culture?
- Love means wanting success for all people in an organization—how are you, personally, stewarding success for people and teams?
- How do you experience resilience in your organization?
- Share a story about a resilient leader or team member—and what you learned from their behaviors.
- How can you develop more resilient leaders?
- What does it look like to unlock innovation inside of your workplace?
- How can you create an environment of belonging within your organization?
- Which pillar of love could you put to work to unlock (a) resilience, (b) belonging, and (c) innovation?
- Thinking practically, what can you start doing immediately to transform your perspective of the bottom line in your organization?
- After reading this chapter, are you skeptical about how behaviors impact the bottom line? If so, share those thoughts with the group.
- What were some of your biggest takeaways or *ah-ha* moments from this chapter?
- Share a moment of self-awareness about your leadership after reading this chapter.
- What, if anything, will you change or adjust about how you lead or behave based on what you've read?

CHAPTER 15

Waiting on the World to Change?

The first time we tried to go Agile back in 2010, we failed.

It's no surprise why. Back then we still followed a command-and-control model. Our leaders would dictate what they wanted to see and then humiliate team members when they messed up. Not only was this cruel, but it wasn't even Agile; our leaders had completely missed the point! It's no surprise, then, that these leaders eventually lost interest and moved on.

The second time we tried to go Agile in 2014, we also failed.

That surprised us. We thought for sure the effort would stick this time. We even had a plan: We would lead with education, winning over our teams' hearts and minds by carefully explaining what Agile was, why it worked so well, and why the transition was so important to our company. Then we would carefully roll it out.

But we forgot one thing: Failure leaves a bitter taste. Many team members still had trauma from the first go-round and weren't interested in trying again. We had the right idea in terms of our communication strategy, but we hadn't considered that the memory of our previous attempt would cast such a long, long shadow.

Actually, we forgot another thing too: Don't roll out a complex organizational change all at once without considering how it would translate to different departments. Each department had different needs and objections. Our creative team, for instance, saw Agile as a software development tool. How could it possibly help them be more productive in their creative work?

We couldn't answer because we hadn't considered their needs. We couldn't answer the concerns of any department. And so it went: Questions stacked on top of questions, fear stacked on top of fear, and our effort to bring Agile to Softway fizzled out once again.

The third time we tried to go Agile in 2020, we finally succeeded.

Why? Because this time, we focused on culture first and learned how to communicate in a way that drives change. Oh, and because we had to. Thanks to that whole COVID-19 pandemic thing that was going on at the time, our backs were against the wall; it was either pivot or die.

Not particularly interested in dying, we added another crucial element to the process to help ensure success: an operating principles document. These operating principles were rooted in Agile but framed in a way that anybody could understand and apply. By focusing on these principles first and the actual Agile processes second, our team members gained a deeper understanding of what we were trying to do. Before they learned the mechanics of Agile, they learned the mindsets that drove it.

Once we had defined our principles, we socialized them every way we could. One of our favorite ways was through a series of short, funny videos. Each video led with a principle, showed how the old Softway would have approached a situation, and then concluded with an example of how the new, Agile Softway would handle it.

This socialization effort achieved two big goals:

1. It simplified the conversation for team members, who now clearly understood what behaviors would need to change.
2. It aligned leadership around these principles so that it drove both our decision making and the language we used to give feedback.

At long last, the change worked—all thanks to a little bit of elbow grease and little bit of love. These days we can easily move people from one stable team to another, if the work calls for it. You could be on one team for several Sprints (an Agile term for a short work cycle) and then be on another team for the next several. Because everyone operates under the same principles and the same culture of love, new teams can get up to speed and begin contributing immediately.

In a culture of love, you know what is required of you. You know you'll be included. You know you'll receive feedback and be asked to give feedback in return. You know that you'll be expected to approach your work in a certain way, no matter whom you're working with.

Before our transformation, this wasn't the case. Our culture was more like the Wild West. Every team had its own culture, leadership style, and way of working. When team members needed to switch teams, it was a major undertaking. For weeks, they would have to sit back and observe how the new team got things done before they could contribute effectively. Sure, we had some bumps along the way as we grew beyond our freewheeling Wild West days, but because trust and feedback are inherent to a culture of love, we were able to work through them.

As we approach the end of the book, you're probably thinking about the challenges inherent in transitioning to a culture of love—or in any big, sweeping transformation, for that matter. We get it. Change is hard. Organizations routinely fail to change—ourselves included.

Fortunately, change is possible. In this chapter, we discuss how to build your own personal case for change and help others do the same. We also discuss communication tools that can help you connect with your people, win them over, and make change stick. Through diligent, consistent, and disciplined work, you can learn how to make sweeping change real and tangible for your team members.

But first, let's consider the question: Why is change so hard?

Why Change Fails

Everyone wants change, but no one wants *to* change.

This isn't just idle chatter. Almost 84 percent of digital and organizational transformations fail.[1] Many of these efforts fail because organizations forget a crucial ingredient: their people. As we said in Chapter 13, change doesn't come through new processes or a new technology stack. Change comes through people and the decisions they make. If leaders are making decisions out of fear, distrust, or a lack of empathy, then those decisions will fail.

Here's how the process usually goes down. The leadership team decides some aspect of the organization needs to change and hammers out the details between its team members. To generate buy-in, the team then states the business case for the organizational change. Maybe the market conditions are changing. Maybe they need to double their revenue. Maybe they want to become the world's leading manufacturer and supplier of Widget X.

Arguing your business case might work for shareholders, but it's not very compelling to other stakeholders. Unless your team members can expect to double their paychecks when the company doubles its revenue, they have little reason to care. Without a reason to care, they see that change as nothing more than an arbitrary corporate goalpost. Why should they make the big and difficult switch when they don't see how it benefits them?

Further compounding the issue, leaders themselves rarely buy into the change. They see it as something the rest of the organization needs to do, but not them. . .just like our leadership the first time we tried to adopt Agile. If you're a leader at your company, remember: Your teams are watching you. If they don't see you practicing what you preach, then they won't bother either.

We know this because we lived it. Our Agile efforts didn't succeed until we were able to:

- ♦ Articulate what this change would mean to every team member and connect their priorities to our larger business case. For a change to take hold, it must feel personal.
- ♦ Develop an actionable change strategy and practice good change hygiene. Leaders must always model what they need from their teams.

And, of course, throw in that extra special ingredient: love.

Now that you understand what *not* to do, let's talk about what *to* do. Our first stop: vision and values.

Start with Vision and Values

Pop quiz time. Right now, off the top of your head, do you know your company's vision and values?

If you're not sure, don't worry—you're far from alone. In fact, if you had asked the average team member what our vision and values were before 2016, they probably wouldn't have been able to tell you either. The reason? Our vision wasn't memorable. See for yourself:

Softway pre-2016: To be the best digital agency and the best technology company in the world.

Our old vision was, well, *fluffy*. It wasn't specific to our company at all, and it wasn't directional. It didn't tell us where to go or how to succeed. It was just an exercise in bland corporate-speak. Our new vision, in our modest opinions, works much better:

Softway post-2016: To bring back humanity to the workplace.

Pivoting to a culture of love meant resetting our vision and setting our eyes on a new path. This wasn't a strategic PR move. It was a reckoning, a chance to ditch the corporate-speak, ask ourselves what we truly believed in, and then rebuild our company on that foundation. To do that, we needed a vision that was specific, inspirational, and uniting. When team members heard our vision, we wanted them to connect with it, to see themselves in it, to be inspired and motivated to fight for that vision every day. Without that personal connection, our culture of love would never be able to reach its full potential.

If the people at your company can't see themselves when they read your vision, rework it. If they can't do that with your new vision either, rework it again—as many times as it takes to get it right.

From there, work to define (or redefine) your values. Values can take on different forms in different organizations. We define our values in our Six Pillars of Love and operating principles. Through these documents, our team members receive clear guidance on how to translate our vision into tangible, consistent behaviors.

That's the key to good values. They must tie in clearly to your vision, they must be specific, and they must be actionable. Skip the consultant-speak. Avoid flat and meaningless words like "integrity," "excellence," and "fairness." They might sound great on paper, but what do they mean? How do you put them into action?

Values are meaningless unless they're tied to behaviors. Our Six Pillars of Love, for instance, describe specific behaviors and examples so our team understands how those values apply in their day-to-day work.

Vision and values have the potential to unite people behind change. They can become the mindsets that drive action. But if there is a misalignment between the values on paper and the actions in reality, your vision and values will only feed mistrust and pushback. Alignment around your vision and values must begin at the senior-most level. As a leader, you must believe in and model the values and the change you want to see. If you can do that successfully, you can begin to generate alignment around your vision and values throughout the organization.

Of course, to begin the process of driving that change, first you need to understand what that change means to you.

Testing Your Values

Have you ever taken the time to compare your company values to the actual written policies in your employee manual? Often those values and policies are in conflict. There is a distinct contrast between what you say you value as an organization and how you choose to operate.

On Chris's first day, he was left in his office by himself with nothing to do. (See Chapter 12.) So, he decided to read through the entire employee handbook and hold it up against our stated values. In the handbook, he noticed a policy that said if any employee was caught sleeping, they would be fired.

But, after just a few weeks on the job, Chris also noticed something else: Everyone took naps at Softway—including Mohammad.

Did this mean Mohammad should be fired from his own company? Of course not. But, according to the handbook, *yes*.

The more he read, the more instances Chris found of policies and procedures that no one was following. Clearly, what Softway *actually* valued versus what it *said* it valued were not aligned.

Successful values should inform your policies and procedures. They should help employees understand how they should behave and what is off limits. If you're unsure whether your values, policies, and procedures are aligned, do what Chris did: Read the dang handbook and find out.

Make a Personal Case for Change

In 2020, the COVID-19 pandemic forced Softway to pivot from our approach as a service-based organization to a products and solutions model. Needless to say, it was a big pivot—and it needed an Agile framework to do it.

The business case for this shift was clear: The new products and services model would offer more opportunities to drive long-term, sustainable revenue at higher margins. Having more forecastability and stability would make it easier to get through uncertain times.

Every big change needs a corresponding business case. But even a good business case is abstract and unlikely to drive people's behaviors. Instead, to drive and champion this change, each member of the leadership team wrote a personal case for change. Here's what the four of us had to say.

FRANK

Frank is motivated by helping people feel less like imposters and more like team members. Frank wants to be part of creating a lasting legacy that will positively impact people, whether that's more financial security for people or a workplace where people experience a deep sense of belonging, unafraid to bring their full selves to work. For Frank, working toward this goal is rejuvenating. He can see the impact that he personally has on the lives around him, even if his name will never be attached to the work.

CHRIS

Chris sees a changing world. The pandemic has made life fundamentally different, and people must adapt. For some people, the change is frightening, but for Chris, it's an open space with limitless opportunities. He can take stock of what works and what doesn't, what he likes and what he doesn't, where he is in his life and where he wants to go, and he can rewrite his future accordingly. To him, change means being able to literally rewrite his destiny. Softway's change becomes part of that.

JEFF

Jeff spends a lot of time connecting with old friends on social media and seeing what they're up to. Too often, he hears stories of how businesses are treating their employees—and none of them are good. He's driven to help change this—even if it's one company or one team at a time. Softway's story and transformation are something that he fully experienced, and it transformed him as well. He knows that the same meaning and purpose can be found for others. Going through his own personal transformation has also made him a better husband, father, and friend—so he's driven to keep focusing and working on himself.

MOHAMMAD

Mohammad has become increasingly invested in spending time with his family in recent years, but juggling his business and his home life has been intense. However, he knows that this intensity is not only unsustainable but unhealthy for his family. Mohammad grew up in a household where his father worked long hours in a toxic workplace just to provide for his kids, and he doesn't want his kids growing up in the same kind of environment. Mohammad knows that many other families struggle with similar problems. If he can solve this problem for others by creating a more stable and predictable environment at Softway, then he can solve it for himself as well, which will afford him the much-needed opportunity to spend time with his children.

What's Your Personal Case for Change?

Now, here's the question: In leading your organization to change to a culture of love, what might your personal case for change look like? What motivates you? What drives you beyond salary or revenue? How does your personal case connect with your business case?

Only you know the answers to these questions. However, we can offer some ideas and starting points, based on the responses from the participants in our Culture Rise events:

- **Leaving a legacy.** Many senior leaders want to be remembered not just for their accomplishments but for how well they treated other people. They're willing to embrace new mindsets and behaviors because they don't want to be remembered as someone people dreaded working with. They want people to come to their funeral.
- **Starting off strong.** Many young leaders are interested in starting off strong. They want to be everyone's best boss and

accomplish great things. They don't want to develop a set of bad behaviors or habits that they'll have to spend the rest of their careers undoing.

◆ **More stability.** Some people just want to come to work each day and be happier. They want to do the right thing and are willing to change whatever is necessary to make going to work something that they look forward to.

◆ **Making amends.** Some leaders said they often misbehaved toward their team members. They would cancel meetings, play mind games, get in shouting matches over trivial issues, and otherwise make others' lives miserable. They wanted to ask for forgiveness so they could be the leaders that people look up to.

◆ **Improving behavior.** Individual contributors wanted to treat their team members better because they saw the impact of their behavior. Referencing our Six Pillars of Love, they would say things like "I want to be more empathetic because I realize that people at work also have lives at home." Or, "I want to make people feel included and give them a safe space to share when they're dealing with something." Rarely did the business case come up.

We hope these examples have sparked a few ideas as you contemplate your own personal case for change. Before trying to bring change to your own organization, take some time to be clear on what this change means for you and your own goals. This personal case for change will allow you to remain on course, do the hard work, and lead by example day by day.

Make Your Case

Still unsure how to write a really great case for change? We've got plenty of change strategy resources to walk you through it at www.LoveAsAStrategy.com/resources.

Communicating Change

Having your business case and your personal case for change is only half the battle. Next you need to communicate that change—what it is, why you're doing it, and *how* you're doing it. After all, it doesn't matter what you intend to do if no one will listen.

What does communicating change look like in a culture of love? Here are the principles we find most important:

- **Know your audience.** Consider the other person's perspective and communicate human to human. When your message is both real and relevant, they will respond.
- **Be relevant and engaging.** No matter what form your message might come in, engage first, teach second. Use plain language, not corporate jargon. Being forceful or dry will do no good. As Chris's sister likes to say, "You gotta give them brownies with their broccoli."
- **Spread the word.** Communicate "to the last seat"—all the way to the people on the front lines.

We've seen the power of this approach not only in our own communications but in the campaigns we've produced for other organizations. For instance, we once created a campaign for one of our energy clients to bring levity to the world of cybersecurity through a series of comedic videos. Our premise was simple yet compelling. Each short featured two characters, one a bad actor trying to launch a cyberattack and the other a clueless employee. In each episode, the employee inevitably lets the bad actor in, and hilarity ensues.

The videos were an instant hit, becoming the most-watched content within the entire organization. The characters even became so popular in Europe that they began showing up on their campus billboards. More important, we proved that it was possible to have brownies with your broccoli. Team members became more cautious about how they checked their email or engaged on social media. Team members even began checking in with cybersecurity before sending out sensitive communications.

Of course, taking the light approach doesn't always work. You would never want to joke around about upcoming layoffs or pay cuts, for instance. To find the right blend of levity, vulnerability, and transparency, know your audience and understand your situation. Here are some other things to keep in mind to nail your change-related communications.

MAKE FAILURE PART OF THE PROCESS

In 2010, Finland introduced the world to the International Day for Failure. Every year on October 13, people are encouraged to share their biggest, most embarrassing slip-ups or failures.

We think this is a great idea. The more we talk about failure, the more we normalize it as a natural part of learning and growth. Just as the doctors and nurses did in Amy Edmondson's landmark study, leaders who share their mistakes demonstrate that it's okay to fail. Seeing this, team members become more willing not only to take risks but to share the results and grow more resilient from the experience.

Speaking openly about failure also humanizes you and makes your message more relatable to your team. After all, change is hard, and you *will* get things wrong. Ask for and receive feedback, and commit to learning from your mistakes. And always remember: It's better to communicate imperfectly than to stay stuck in silence.

MAKE IT ABOUT PEOPLE

In one 7,000-person organization we worked with, the senior leaders behaved like gods on Olympus, aloof and removed from the everyday world. Rank-and-file workers knew nothing about them as people. Was the VP married? Did he have kids? Where was he from? No one knew.

It was our job to change that. So, we created a campaign where we interviewed leaders for five to seven minutes apiece, not about work but about *them.* We asked where they went to school, what their friends were like, who their family was, what their favorite TV shows were, and so on. Sometimes we ate ice cream with them. Other times we hosted push-up competitions. Whatever it took to give the conversation a taste of authenticity.

After the videos were released, the difference was immediate. For instance, once everyone learned that one VP was a big *Game of Thrones* fan, people regularly stopped him in the hallways to chat about the latest episode. Immediately, the perception of this VP went from stuffy and stoic to human and approachable.

This kind of vulnerable, human-interest focus may just feel like filler, but it is everything to the health of an organization—especially one in the middle of a transformation. After all, many of us spend more time with our fellow team members than we do with our own friends and family. Do we *really* want to spend so much of that time with complete strangers? Nearly any message will be more engaging, more memorable, and more effective in making a case for change when it's delivered by someone you know.

BE TRANSPARENT (TO A DEGREE)

Transparency has been a big buzzword for years now. And for good reason: It positively affects business outcomes. For example, research shows that people will make more responsible cost decisions if they can see the impact on the bottom line.

That said, especially when it comes to communicating for change, it is possible to be too transparent.

Leaders are sometimes under great pressure to share information, but if they share too little information too soon, it doesn't help anyone. Why?

- ◆ Incomplete information often leads to a barrage of unanswerable questions.
- ◆ Incomplete information can cause people to lose faith in a planned or in-progress change effort.
- ◆ Incomplete information can cause people to make up their own answers to fill in the gaps. After all, Nature abhors a vacuum. Unfortunately, these back-channel conversations only lead to more instability and fear.

When the full truth finally does arrive after incomplete information has been shared, even though you and your team were careful in your planning, many will still distrust it. You may have thought you were committing an act of love by sharing incomplete information early. In reality, you committed an act of sabotage in terms of time, energy, and focus.

For instance, you know those first two attempts to switch to Agile that didn't pan out? Well, those misfires led to several hours of one-on-ones and team meetings to clean up the damage and reassure the many, many anxious team members throughout the organization who were worried we were headed in the wrong direction. That's time and emotional capital that we'll never get back.

Responsible transparency recognizes that there are different degrees of information sharing. For instance, let's say your company is about to undergo a reorganization. Reorgs usually take several months of careful planning across divisions, and ultimately they affect everyone's job. Naturally, when people know a reorg is coming, they'll want to know what it means for them—even before you have the answers.

In such a situation, you can do two things.

1. You can fudge it and leave your team members with a growing sense of uncertainty and dread.
2. You can be transparent about the fact that you're not ready to answer the question yet.

We recommend door number two. Here, while you're transparent that there will indeed be changes, you're also clear that you're still in the process of gathering information before you can share any updates. By managing expectations, you demonstrate that you and the organization are not approaching the reorg in a haphazard way.

Of course, at times immediate transparency is the best call, even if you don't know all the answers. At the outset of the COVID-19 pandemic, when we were losing literally millions of dollars in canceled contracts, it would have been strange if we hadn't spoken up. Instead, we got in front of the situation and made ourselves available to answer any questions team members had or to discuss how the pandemic was impacting them personally. In moments like these, you'll see your investment in culture pay off tenfold.

Leadership and Communication

When you're a leader, receiving communication can sometimes feel as if you're getting a watermelon. It's green on the outside, so it looks good. But then, you open it up to find out it's red. The information is far from good—in fact, the world is on fire!

(continued)

Your team members may mean well, but often they're inclined to deliver news in a way they think their leaders want to hear it. As a result, finding the truth can be an exercise in disappointment and frustration.

To get accurate information and to understand what your people need to hear and how, it's important to build a network of people who will tell you the truth without sugarcoating—people who understand how your teams are doing, what they're experiencing, and what their needs are. By learning to take the temperature of the room more effectively, you can respond with empathy—and without losing track of your goal among the details.

Ask questions. Get feedback. Speak with your listeners in mind. But above all, be persistent. Don't let the fact that your team might be overthinking their message stop you from getting at the truth.

Building Change Networks

Every political movement requires grassroots organization. A community must knock on doors, raise money, facilitate communications, and set up meetings with special-interest groups to turn out the vote. Similarly, organizations depend on grassroots internal change networks to help drive any new initiative.

Change networks influence individual team members to behave differently, manage differently, and even be led differently. As we saw with our attempts to go Agile, this is no easy task. After all, change requires a large group of people to be convinced, one by one, to become believers. Even the most charismatic leaders can't achieve all this change by themselves. The true work of change begins when you have built a network of people within the company who are all committed to helping you champion the change.

When recruiting change agents to your network, here are some traits to look for:

- ◆ People who naturally have the gift of speaking truth to power
- ◆ Influencers who are good at convincing others to be uncomfortable and take smart risks

- Pioneers who are always looking for the best path forward
- Communicators who are good go-betweens for teams and leadership
- Team members with a finger on the pulse of internal chatter—who know how organizational messages are being received (and how you might want to adjust going forward)

Change networks don't just help get the word out. They also bring the word back to leadership. In other words, they create a positive feedback loop that helps leadership, their teams, and the organization become more aligned.

Although change networks tend to grow organically, they also need to be maintained. The effort to do so isn't one-and-done. Change networks require maintenance—and you neglect their care at your own peril.

The big reason for this dynamic is good, old-fashioned human skepticism. Just because you've committed your organization to go all in on Love as a Business Strategy, it doesn't mean everyone is going to jump on the love horse and ride off into the sunset with you. Even after our pivot to a culture of love, we still encounter skepticism with every new change effort.

That's okay. Be kind to your skeptics. Don't treat them like barnacles to be scraped off the hull. Instead, treat them as allies.

No, really. Skeptics are people who have not yet understood the value of what you're trying to do. They are naturally going to inquire, test, seek validation, and do research, and others are going to learn from their example. In other words, skeptics mobilize people—and that's a good thing! Your job is to listen when they raise valid concerns and speak honestly about your personal reasons for change.

This principle is why we put so much emphasis on building your personal case for change earlier in the chapter. Before anyone else believes, *you* must believe. Before anyone else walks the walk, *you* must walk the walk. Before anyone else evangelizes the change effort, *you* must evangelize the change effort.

So don't be afraid of skeptics. Embrace them. Share with them. Get to the bottom of their concerns. Talk about your organization's new vocabulary for a culture of love—words like "introspection," "forgiveness," "empathy," and "trust." Share what the words mean both to you and to the organization. Ask the skeptics what risks they see in treating people better.

Then walk them through the reality of what a better workplace could look like. Ask them to imagine how it could make their lives—and their teammates' lives—better. Then (and only then) explain the business case, discussing the improved outcomes of high-performing teams and how that will lead to more innovation, more revenue, lower turnover, and so on.

Make the case, one skeptic at a time. If you can convince and convert them, they will become your biggest advocates.

Proof in Action

In the business world, when people consider change, their minds almost immediately turn to metrics and data. We value these tools as well, but we see them as part of a more holistic view of change. Far too often organizations attempt a change, look at a narrow band of data and metrics, and get frustrated when they see middling results.

If you're only looking for quick results, hire a consulting firm to retool your values and launch a PR campaign around them. Just don't expect whatever bump you get to last.

However, if you're looking to create lasting change, you must be willing to put in deep, sustained work for a long time before you see any measurable results at all.

Think all the way back to the introduction to Part I, where we described our philosophy of love. There's a reason we modeled that philosophy like a building: foundation first, then supporting infrastructure, and then the finishing touches. Although the first two parts are the most important, it's the third part that everybody notices.

If you put in the work, you'll get there. Others *will* notice and validate your hard work. Just be patient.

We were nearly two years into our transformation before our customers noticed the difference in our culture. But once they did notice the change, they saw it everywhere. They saw it in how our teams performed. They saw it in the way we communicated both with them and with each other—always with kindness and respect. They saw the ideas we brought to the table. They saw it in Mohammad, in Softway's leaders, and in every single team they interacted with.

Perhaps most noticeably, they saw it in the outcomes we created for them. This awareness of our effort led to a virtuous cycle. Because our culture of love got results, our customers trusted us more. Because they trusted us more, they partnered with us on larger, more complex, and more lucrative projects. Because they partnered with us on these projects, we produced increasingly better results. And so on.

As you well know, your customers can be your biggest skeptics. But our customers couldn't deny the results. They saw the transformation we had gone through, they saw the difference it made in how we approached our work, and they wanted it for themselves. So, one day, they asked us to teach them how we did it. After a messy but successful pilot, the Culture Rise leadership experience was born. (See Chapter 8.)

These days, Culture Rise has helped us teach Love as a Business Strategy to thousands of business leaders across the world. (We've even written a book about it!) But at the time, we were in uncharted territory. We'd never consulted in the transformation space—or even imagined that we would. We'd gone through our own transformation to a culture of love purely out of need. Now that we had emerged victorious, we were happy to seize on this new (and unexpected) business opportunity.

But we were terrified of screwing it up.

For the next several weeks, everyone in the organization stepped up to make sure we not only proved the value of a culture of love but also created a presentation that was truly special. Those were a few tense weeks: Not everybody on our clients' executive leadership team was on board.

Remember what we said in the first chapter: Love is speaking truth to power. Rather than shrink at our clients' objections, we challenged them. In one exercise, we had members of their team write anonymous letters about the organization's leadership. Then we asked the executive leadership team to read those letters aloud to each other. They were absolutely floored by the results. Suddenly those skeptics realized that they might just be able to learn a thing or two from us.

That victory got us to the next step: a one-off workshop at the company's branch office in South America. Afterward, the executive leadership team brought us back and asked their people on the ground whether they should continue to roll out our Culture Rise training. Participants had enjoyed the experience so thoroughly—and received so much value from it—that they demanded it be rolled out for the entire company.

We didn't ask for this full-throated approval, but we were sure happy to get it.

Soon the company had funded a multimillion-dollar program based solely on the impact it had seen during that one workshop in South America.

Nothing will convince a skeptic faster than consistent behavior change and consistent results. But it takes time. Don't focus on their short-term objections. Focus on how you can connect with these skeptics instead. How can you make your change personal? How can you demonstrate results? How can you communicate in a way that is not only engaging and compelling but also informative and valuable? In other words, how can you sneak the broccoli into the brownie?

Change *is* possible, but your words and behaviors are what will convince people to change.

Ultimately, that is the best kind of proof—the proof in action.

Questions for "Waiting on the World to Change?"

- ◆ Share how this book has reframed your understanding of culture in the workplace.
- ◆ What role do you play in creating the right environment for culture to flourish?
- ◆ Have you been a part of a pivot-or-die moment in your organization or on your team? Share that experience.
- ◆ Why do you think previous change initiatives have failed in this (or previous) organizations?
- ◆ What's the secret sauce for change efforts to be successful?
- ◆ Share your company's vision and values with the group (to the best of your memory).
- ◆ Thinking practically, how can you link your organization's values to behaviors? How can you start living those behaviors?
- ◆ Take some time to think about your own personal case for change. What motivates you? What drives you beyond just salary and title? Share it with the group.

- How could your organization embrace "responsible transparency" when communicating internally?
- Share some examples where transparency wasn't shared from leadership. What were the implications?
- Thinking practically, what can you start doing immediately to transform your organization's communications strategy?
- After reading this chapter, are you skeptical about the topics shared? If so, share those thoughts with the group.
- How are you demonstrating proof in action?
- What were some of your biggest takeaways or *ah-ha* moments from this chapter?
- Share a moment of self-awareness about your leadership after reading this chapter.
- What, if anything, will you change or adjust about how you lead or behave based on what you've read?

Note

1. Phil Lewis, "Where Businesses Go Wrong with Digital Transformation," *Forbes*, July 31, 2019. www.forbes.com/sites/phillewis1/2019/07/31/where-businesses-go-wrong-with-digital-transformation/?sh=31fd8cf670bb

CHAPTER 16

No More Excuses

Now that you've reached the final chapter, we're going to make a prediction.

As you were reading this book, there was a little voice in your head reading along with you. With each new story you read, with each new concept you learned, that voice tried to convince you to quit before you even began:

> "Sure, that worked for them, but that would never work in our company."
> "I could never get leadership to commit to this."
> "This is way more effort than I can handle right now."

Sound familiar? Whatever that voice said, it was speaking in the language of a fixed mindset. The question is, are you going to listen to it?

Right now, you have two paths.

1. Close the book, put it back on your shelf, and never think about it again.
2. Commit to adopting a culture of love in your organization, and share this book with everyone you can think of.

Path 1 is easier, but it's also a dead end. Path 2 will set you and your organization on a journey of profound personal and professional transformation, but it will require sacrifice and hard work.

So, which path will you choose?

Naturally, you know which path we *hope* you will choose. But before you make your choice, let's take a moment to quiet that voice of objection rattling around in your head.

The next excuses are the most common ones we hear from the many organizations, leaders, and team members when we discuss Love as a Business Strategy. If we're honest, they're also the same excuses we said and heard when *we* started out on this journey.

We never said love was going to be easy. In fact, throughout this book, we've said the exact opposite. But here's the thing: Nearly everything worth doing both in life and in business is hard. Only by embracing the challenge and confronting these excuses can we move past them.

So buckle up. It's time for some tough love.

Excuse #1: Other Culture Initiatives Didn't Work

We get these "been there, done that" responses a lot. At their core, these objections are rooted in lack of forgiveness for failed past initiatives. Maybe a trainer came to the office and ran a workshop. Maybe the executive leadership team attended a weekend seminar. Or maybe a consultant came and made a sincere effort to reshape the organization.

Whatever the specifics, the effort didn't work.

But just because something didn't work out doesn't mean you should stop trying. It doesn't mean change *can't* occur.

Our failed initiatives that have taught us the most. Look at how much we learned about communication and leading change in our three attempts to go Agile. With each failure, we took our lumps, learned our lessons, and made a better effort next time.

Culture-based initiatives could fail for a number of reasons. In our opinion, most fail because they don't focus on meaningful change to begin with. Maybe the organization dusted off their value statements or designed new policies around diversity and inclusion. Well-intentioned efforts like this fail to get at the root problem: behaviors.

However, when you focus on behaviors, a funny thing happens: The initiative is no longer about success or failure. It's about progress.

Excuse #2: We Can't Afford It

Let's call this excuse what it is: a smokescreen. When someone says, "I can't afford it," they're really saying "That's not important to me." They're scared. They're inflexible. They're consumed by that old-school corporate mentality of profit over people.

Leaders with this mindset will burn through money chasing new revenue opportunities. And yet the second someone utters the word *culture*, suddenly they're tightening their purse strings and quoting revenue forecasts.

Let's be clear on two things.

1. The most important thing in your business is your people. Period.
2. If you truly want something, you'll find the budget to pay for it. We're all rational to a degree, but often our money decisions come down to what we need or want at the moment.

We get it: Culture transformations can be both expensive and time-consuming. Yes, it takes money to hire consultants. Yes, it takes money to attend seminars. Yes, it costs money to properly train and onboard your employees, to make them feel included, and to pay the additional cost for business-class tickets. Think of these expenses not as costs but as *investments* that, when, executed with love and intention, can pay off tenfold.

Don't believe us? Here's what we want you to do. First, ask yourself about all the costs you're ignoring—the cost of a high attrition rate, the cost of having little to no repeat business, and the cost of unaligned, ineffective teams. If you can, put a number to those costs—even if it's just a ballpark estimate.

Next, ask yourself how much more you can profit from a high-performing team, how many more revenue opportunities you'll earn through repeat business and word of mouth, and how much time you save when your leaders and your team members are aligned. Again, if you can, put a number to the value of those business outcomes.

Now look at the two numbers side by side. Still think it's not worth the investment?

Behaviors *are* the bottom line. The return on investment of culture manifests in improved behaviors—and behaviors are what shift the numbers on the balance sheet. When you choose people over profit, your people choose you. The reward in improved business outcomes will more than make the investment worth it.

Excuse #3: Change Is Too Hard

The average person spends over 90,000 hours at work. Those in leadership positions often spend much more than that.

Yes, change is hard. But do you know what's harder?

Spending 90,000 hours in misery because you didn't speak up.

There's a big difference between being hard and being impossible. In our experience, the biggest difference between success and failure has nothing to do with the size of the challenge and everything to do with commitment. The more you are willing to commit, the more likely you are to succeed. It really is that simple.

Commitment is the hardest step on the path to change because it's the first. From there, each step gets a little easier. And the farther down the path you go, the more you realize you're not alone. After all, if commitment is anything, it's contagious. Once others see what you're trying to create, many will fall into step right alongside you.

Excuse #4: Change Takes Too Long

Today's business landscape is much different than it was in 2000, 2010, or even—dare we mention it—2020. Things happen faster. Every decision must be made yesterday. Course corrections must come swiftly and confidently.

That's what we're made to believe anyway. It's easy to get caught up in the instant gratification game, but the truth is, change still takes time. If you pull the plug on an important initiative before it has a chance to work its magic, you do so at your own peril.

Creating a culture of love doesn't happen in a day, a week, or even a year. It happens in small steps, in daily repetitions, in every moment of introspection where you commit to doing right by the people around you.

Changing the behavior of one person is challenging and messy. Changing the behavior of an entire organization is even messier. Boundaries will get pushed. Relationships will be tested. Surprises will happen. But if you want lasting change, you must be willing to let these processes unfold at their own pace. If you try to rush things along—or, worse, if you give up before you begin to see the results—you risk doing irreparable harm to your organizational culture. If you do, folks won't trust you—they won't care. And they'll be harder to convince the next time you try to roll something out.

Excuse #5: I'm Not in a Leadership Role

Everyone has a chance to make a difference in their organization. You may not be a leader *yet*, but don't you want to get there eventually? Why not create some momentum around that intention by promoting a culture of love?

Here's some real tough love: If you're not willing to stand up for a better culture in your workplace, then you might as well stop complaining and get back to work. And if you *are* willing to stand up for a better culture and you get fired for it, then you probably shouldn't be working there in the first place. (Please let us know if you do get fired. If so, [1] sorry not sorry, and [2] we'd love to meet you.)

With that said, here's a word of encouragement. If you're a middle manager, you're in the perfect position to drive change from within.

Why? Because of a little thing we lovingly call the *crap umbrella*.

Middle managers take a lot of crap. In a fear-based organization, that crap is raining down on them day in and day out. It's gross—but not inevitable.

When you embrace a culture of love, you get all the fringe benefits that come with it—including your very own crap umbrella. All you have to do is hold it over your head, open it up, and *voilà*—you and your team are now protected from all the daily crap that has been raining down on you.

That's a big deal. After all, it's easy to think that you don't have any influence as a middle manager. But to your team, you *are* the leader. *You* call the shots as far as their lives are concerned. Armed with your trusty crap umbrella, you can build an ecosystem of empathy, trust, and vulnerability for your team—so they don't have to deal with any of the s*** you're dealing with. And once your team knows that you're there to protect them, not only will they be willing to move mountains, but they'll be ready to open their own crap umbrellas wide to extend your impact. If enough people do this, then one day, just maybe, that rain of crap might cease altogether.

Excuse #6: Things Aren't That Bad

This excuse is the most dangerous of them all—the biggest, most diabolical lie that leaders tell themselves. But ask yourself this: If things *really* aren't that bad, why did you read this book all the way to the end?

Here's the truth. In a fear-based organization, when things go bad, leaders are usually the last to know. By the time it reaches them, all the bad news has been rebranded to look like good news. So, when you say "Things aren't that bad," all you're really saying is that you're out of touch. And the moment your team members realize this, they will start formulating an exit strategy.

Besides, even if you know things are going just okay, how long do you think "okay" is going to last? How long can you remain stagnant without losing ground in your market?

Maybe for a little while. But not forever.

We get it: Sometimes it feels safer to cling to the illusion that the problems you know are better than the problems you don't. In reality, though, staying put is often a much bigger risk. We stayed put for years, and it almost bankrupted us.

You don't have to be like us. You have an opportunity to change course now before the problems grow any worse.

The Time Is Now

What you're feeling right now is the residual effect of tough love. It might not feel like it now, but that sting is good. If you remember way back in Chapter 1 and Chapter 2, we said that if you want to create a culture of love, then you've got to lean into the hard talks so you can build a path forward.

For too long, the corporate world has been stuck in old, outdated mindsets and unwilling to change. Today, whether we like it or not, that change is upon us. Business as usual isn't good enough anymore. The organizations that accept this fact and embrace a culture of love will be best positioned not only to adapt and survive but to thrive in the face of whatever big change the world throws our way next.

When we struggle together, we learn together. When we learn together, we succeed together. Embracing our basic humanity and approaching our work with inclusion, trust, and empathy isn't a sign of weakness. It's a sign of strength.

But change starts with you. If this is the future you want, then create it.

No matter your role, no matter the current culture of your team, *you* have the ability to change. It's a big task, but, like any big task, it can be achieved in small steps. Here are the two most important steps to get started.

STEP #1: KNOW YOUR "WHY"

It's easy to think of change as a *what*. But look deeper. Lasting change always begins with *why*.

Everyone's *why* is different—and understanding yours requires self-awareness and introspection. To get there, ask:

- Why do you need change? Why should you adopt new policies or practice the principles of leadership?
- Whom is this change for, a specific team or your entire organization?
- If you could create an environment that was inclusive, supportive, and sustainable, what would that look like?
- Why is this change worth it to you? To your company? To your employees and their families?
- How do you want to be remembered? How can you change to help bring this about?
- What would drive your team members to wake up every day and be excited to be a part of your team? What do they need to know to trust the change you're attempting to create? How can they be confident that the effort will pay off in the end?

Knowing your *why* is Step #1. It's the foundation that a culture of love is built upon. It's your motivator to keep pushing forward—the superpower that will help you see past the small roadblocks and continue full speed ahead.

You might know your *why* already. If you don't, start by asking yourself what change you want to see in your organization and why that's important to you. Start conversations with other leaders or team members. Share what you're thinking and invite their feedback. If you keep doing your work, your *why* will come to you—and if it changes as you move ahead, that's okay too.

STEP #2: MAKE MICRO-COMMITMENTS

Once you know your *why*, the next step is to start moving. Just remember, change never comes all at once.

It might feel good to set out with a big, all-encompassing, life-changing goal, but we recommend a different approach: Start small, make micro-commitments, and follow through. Over time, these small, incremental improvements will lead to big change.

When we say *micro-commitments*, we mean it. Itty-bitty baby steps. Create a goal so tiny, so seemingly insignificant, so atomic a habit that you'll have no excuse not to check it off your list. And be specific—clear, actionable micro-commitments only.

For instance, it's much easier to commit to writing a single thank-you note than it is to "build better relationships." The latter is so vague you won't know where to start (and often won't). The former commitment is specific and contained—and you'll know full well whether you accomplished it.

That's the beauty of micro-commitments: By putting yourself in a position to succeed, you *will* succeed. And you'll be much, much more likely to keep the effort going.

Once you've created a micro-commitment and made it a habit or checked it off your list, commit to another. And then another after that. And another after that. And so on.

Through micro-commitments, we were able to turn the big ideas of love as a business strategy into small, daily wins. A culture of love is a mammoth idea. It has taken us years to turn this big idea into everyday reality. But the more micro-commitments we made, the more we celebrated the daily wins, the more our efforts snowballed into something bigger.

That's how a culture of love is built. Not in a day, but through everyday effort.

A New Reality Is Possible

Our stated mission is to bring humanity back to the workplace. When many hear this, they're incredulous. What does that even mean? How is that even possible? Why would we even try to do that? Isn't the point of business to make money, not sing songs around a campfire? Why even bother?

Here's why: because business is personal.

For too long, we working professionals have brushed off the toxic cultures endemic in so many organizations. When someone is belittled, dehumanized, or fired, we say it's business as usual. As long as we tell ourselves this lie, then we are bound to it. That is our reality.

But it doesn't have to be. There is an alternative reality.

A reality where you can bring your full self to work, where you look forward to going to work, where you don't get the "Sunday scaries."

A reality where having a good time and being productive isn't mutually exclusive, where you know you can count on your team members for support, where team members strive to do their best work—not because they're afraid, but because they *enjoy it.*

A reality where your company truly cares about your well-being, where you have a purpose and feel valued and respected, where you can grow, learn, and thrive.

A reality where you are valued for your difference in opinion, where there is no difference in "work you" and "home you," where you're included regardless of ethnicity, education, religion, gender, country of origin, or political affiliation.

That is the reality we aspire to. That is the reality we work every day to create. That is the reality that the many other organizations we've worked with have embraced.

That can be your reality too. A reality where love is your business strategy.

If you're ready, we invite you to join us.

Getting Started

As the old saying goes, "The best time to plant a tree was twenty years ago. The second-best time is now."

It's time to plant your tree and take a stand for love.

To help you on your journey, we've created a handy worksheet that will teach you everything you need to know about micro-commitments.

For the worksheet and many more resources to help you adopt love as a business strategy (including our first-in-the-universe Culture Counter tool), visit www.LoveAsAStrategy .com/resources.

Questions for "No More Excuses"

- ◆ Be honest: Did you find yourself agreeing with one of the excuses listed in this chapter? If so, why?
- ◆ Share a few ideas about overcoming these excuses.
- ◆ What other excuses have you heard about why behavior/culture change doesn't work?
- ◆ What are some ways you could convince leadership to consider going on this journey?
- ◆ What steps can you take to make a positive impact in your workplace?
- ◆ What may be holding you back from committing to change?
- ◆ Share a story about how you've put up the crap umbrella for others.
- ◆ When have people put up the crap umbrella for you?
- ◆ Introspective question: What would it take for you to be the change you wish to see?
- ◆ If you're committed, how are you going to see this transformation come to fruition?
- ◆ Thinking practically, what can you start doing immediately to transform the communications strategy in your organization?
- ◆ After reading this chapter, are you skeptical about the topics shared? If so, share those thoughts with the group.

- What were some of your biggest takeaways or *ah-ha* moments from this chapter?
- Share a moment of self-awareness about your leadership after reading this chapter.

Closing Out Part III

- Consider your workplace. Which part of your organization embraces "love" the most?
- Share some ways you could see your team embracing love as a business strategy. What changes are needed to make this a reality?
- Consider the processes and policies you have in place today. Which ones could be antithetical to a culture of love?
- Are your organization's values being showcased through behaviors, or are they just words on a poster? How can you bring these values to life?
- What stories in Part III resonated with you the most? Why?
- What lessons from Part III are you going to start incorporating in the way you lead others?

One More Thing

Thank you so much for taking the time to read our book and have honest/courageous conversations about it as a group.

It means the world to us.

To that end, we'd like to offer you (and your book club) something in return.

Once you finish the book together, we'd love to schedule a virtual meeting with your book club to answer any questions you may have for us. Ask us anything. No joke.

Just send an email to laabs@softway.com and we'll schedule some time to meet.

Thank you for helping us bring humanity back to the workplace!

Acknowledgments

First and foremost, we would like to thank Softway employees, past and present. To every person who has been a part of our company, every client, partner, and friend—thank you for being part of Softway's journey and for your dedication and support. To the folks who made this book possible, thank you. Chas Hoppe in particular, this book would not have been possible without your support and expertise.

From Mohammad Anwar

This book wouldn't exist without the amazing collaboration of Chris Pitre, Frank Danna, and Jeff Ma. Thank you all for jumping into this crazy adventure with me. Your passion, dedication, and willingness to share your stories, experiences, and expertise made the entire process a joy. I'm so grateful to have you as my coauthors and partners in crime here at Softway!

Shakila Begum and Abdul Anwar (Mom and Dad)—To my parents, I am extremely grateful and forever indebted to you both for all of your sacrifices and hard work that you've put in for our entire family and me. I am so grateful for the values you instilled in me and the effort it took to set a great example for how to live and lead my life. Love you, Mom and Dad!

Khaleel Anwar (Big Bro), Faizun Anwar (Sis), Taj Anwar (Bro), Siraj Anwar (Bro)—I want to thank all four of my elder siblings for being my role models and protectors, and for being there for me no matter what I wanted to do. Your trust in me to lead Softway has allowed me to learn so much, and I will always be grateful to all of you for forgiving me for all the mistakes and blunders I have made along the way. Thank you, love you all!

Yulia Pakhalina (Spouse)—Thank you to my beautiful wife! Many people may not see the sacrifices and the effort you put in to make sure that I am able to pursue my dreams with Softway, but I want you to know that I am eternally grateful for you and everything you do for our children and me. Without your support and cooperation, there wouldn't be a Softway. This journey thus far wouldn't have even been possible. Behind every successful man is a great woman. That great woman is you, Yulia. Without you I wouldn't be able to achieve any of the success or continue to do so in the future. Thank you, love you!

Sufia Anwar and Mohsin Anwar (Children)—You have made me a better father, person, and human. Raising both of you has been an incredible joy and I look forward to what the future holds for both of you. Thank you for your unconditional love and support in everything that I set out to do. Love you both loads!

Waqar Faiz (Mentor)—Thank you to my spiritual mentor, Waqar Faiz, for teaching me plenty of life lessons and for giving me a chance to introspect on my behaviors. Thank you for always being there to listen to me, hear me out, and give me the confidence and belief in anything that I needed to do. I am forever grateful for all of your teachings and encouragement.

Softway's past employees—To all the employees who have ever worked at Softway, thank you for your services and dedication. Thank you for giving me an opportunity to lead you all, but, most important, I want to apologize to each and every one of you if I have hurt you or mistreated you (knowingly or unknowingly). I am grateful to each and every person who has been a part of Softway. You helped shape my perspective on my leadership and who I am as a person. Thank you!

Softway's current employees—To all the current employees who are by my side as we go forward on this journey to try to bring back humanity to the workplace: thank you! Thank you for having faith and belief in our vision and purpose at Softway. Without you, I wouldn't even be a leader in the first place. I wouldn't be able to keep on this journey without all of your support, but also without you holding me accountable and always being real with me and letting me hear what I really needed to hear. I am forever grateful to you all for your commitment, sacrifices, and hard work in this journey of ours! Thank you and love you all!

Customers, past and present—Thank you to all of our past and present clients. Thank you for entrusting Softway and me with solving problems and creating solutions for your organizations and teams. We value the opportunity you have given us and continue to give us to serve you and your team. I personally have learned a lot from each and every one of you. You all have been mentors to me in more ways than you know.

Coach Tom Herman—Coach, I have never spoken with you or met you! I don't know if I'll ever have a chance to meet with you, but you have been my mentor from the moment I saw you speak at a press conference on November 17, 2015, when you spoke about your win as head coach of the University of Houston after their victory over the University of Memphis Tigers. You taught me about a culture of love and what it means to be resilient and love your teammates. You gave me faith, hope, and belief for my own company and over 160 employees at that time when we didn't even know if we would survive and succeed or if our company would shut down or go bankrupt. I don't know if we would have survived as a business and thrived if it wasn't for your speech that day. I have watched you and modeled my own style of leadership and was inspired to create a culture of love inside our business because of you. You have helped me and our business in ways that you cannot imagine. But if you ever do read this book, I hope that you can see how much of an impact you have made on complete strangers—even off the field. I will forever be grateful to you and will be your fan for life—because you changed my life and so many others. Thank you, Coach!

From Frank Danna

It's always been a dream of mine to write a book, a dream that started with me watching in awe as my late father, Charles Danna, furiously scribbled away at his manuscripts. He died before he was able to publish his novel, so Dad—thank you for inspiring me. 'There is no box'.

To my wife—Megan, you are the most incredible person I've ever met. Your kindness, honesty, love, bravery, and brilliance are legendary. Over our incredible journey thus far, you've made me a better person and a better father. I married so far out of my league, y'all.

To my children—Emma and Levi, I love you so much. You both make life worth living. Life is more colorful, joyful, and fun with you in it. I can't wait to see how each of you changes the world.

To Mohammad—You saw something in me that others didn't. You supported me from the sidelines, gave me chances when no one else would, and showed me what real inclusion looks and feels like. You taught me to pay opportunity forward. I won't let you down. Thank you for your friendship, and thank you for Softway.

To my coauthors—Jeff, Chris, and Mohammad—you're not colleagues, you're family. The shade, the laughs, the heartbreak, and the triumph. We've been there for each other through thick and thin. Like the quality and craftsmanship of a pair of Adidas shoes, our bond will last a lifetime.

To everyone at Softway, past and present—I love you all. Thank you for your dedication to this company and the work we're doing.

To my parents (all of you, my amazing in-laws included)—Your support and encouragement are incredible. Thank you for believing in me.

To my family and friends—The unconditional love that you share keeps me motivated.

Finally, to you, the reader of this book—You've taken time out of your life to learn a little more about our journey, and I hope you found real value in our stories and lessons. Thank you so much!

From Jeff Ma

Every lesson in this book is deeply rooted in my personal journey. I've faced difficult conversations, endured painful introspection, and wrestled with some truly flawed behavior in my effort to transform over the past few years.

> **My incredible wife, Maggie**—Whether I was at my best or my worst, she held my hand—both literally and figuratively—never turning away, always lifting me up. Maggie, your grace, patience, and unwavering love are the foundation of everything I've accomplished. I couldn't have made it here without you. Thank you from the depths of my heart.
>
> **My coauthors**—You are more than colleagues; you are brothers-in-arms. We've weathered the trenches together, and your unyielding support has meant everything. A special thank-you to Mohammad, who always saw the good in me, even when I struggled to see it in myself. Your belief in me has been a guiding light.
>
> **My children, Cody and Penny**—You inspire me every day. Your curiosity, resilience, and joy have taught me more than I could ever hope to teach you. In ways big and small, you've shown me what it means to grow, to love, and to keep pushing forward. I am endlessly proud of both of you, and I hope this book reflects even a fraction of what you've given me.

From Chris Pitre

There is no such thing as a self-made man. Along with the many men who have supported and helped (including my father, Arthur D. Pitre, and my coauthors), I am especially grateful for the women who have poured into me. To the five women who have shaped my professional and personal conscience:

> **Alice Pitre**—My mom. The one who instilled in me the importance of detail orientation and efficiency in chores, education, and life.
>
> **Phyllis Wiggins**—My pastor. The one who blessed me with wisdom, faith, and my first dose of introspection.

Kandace Cooks—My sister. The one who taught me how to write, laugh, and lead. (This is the only place I'll admit that you taught me how to write.)

Dr. Lynda Maddox—My favorite professor. The one who taught me the importance of self-editing, strategy, and the power of storytelling.

Rebecca Rogers Tijerino—My first executive mentor. The one who trained me in the art of selling, understanding financials, and ensuring alignment.

About the Authors

As a result of Softway's cultural transformation, Mohammad, Chris, Frank, and Jeff co-founded Culture+ (culture-plus.com) and co-created the Culture Rise training experience, along with other culture-based products, services, and experiences. *Love as a Business Strategy*, now in its second edition, is each author's debut book.

Mohammad F. Anwar

Mohammad is the youngest of five children and was born and raised in Saudi Arabia by Indian parents from Bengaluru. He graduated from the University of Houston (Go, Coogs) with a BS in Computer Science and started Softway at age 20, where he still serves as president and CEO.

Mohammad lives in Sugar Land, Texas, with his amazing wife, Yulia, a Russian diver and five-time Olympic medalist, and his beautiful children, Sufia and Mohsin. In his spare time, he enjoys fitness, watching college sports, and butchering American idioms.

Frank E. Danna

Frank, the oldest of six children, can often be found perfecting the art of brewing, drinking, and sharing coffee with friends and family. Frank is an entrepreneur at heart, having successfully sold his first startup at age 25.

Frank is a pop culture connoisseur, world traveler, and citizen of Disneyland. In his spare time, he bakes award-winning cookies, makes silly videos, and enjoys fitness (to offset the cookies). Frank lives in Houston, Texas, with his gorgeous wife, Megan, and awesome children, Emma and Levi.

Jeffrey F. Ma

Jeff spent the first decade of his career working in the video game industry, from game testing to project management. He continues to bring his love for games into everything he does, from playing with his kids to training and coaching leaders.

Jeff has a burning passion for board games, magic tricks, Agile, and growth mindsets. He was born and raised in Texas, where he and his beautiful wife, Maggie, dote on their wonderful children, Cody and Penelope.

Christopher J. Pitre

Chris is a student of the world and enjoys anthropology, history, travel, and culinary experiences. His interests in global cultures naturally led him to travel around the world, cofacilitating Culture Rise, a leadership development training program, and managing client relationships globally. Chris is a native Houstonian who loves everything Beyoncé. He has a BA in Business Administration from The George Washington University in Washington, DC.

About Softway

Softway is a people first consulting firm that helps evolving businesses transform in areas of technology, communication, and culture.

In 2021, after Softway's dramatic cultural change, Culture+ was co-founded to bring culture and leadership products, training, and consulting to their clients.

In 2015, when a toxic culture almost bankrupted the company, Softway's leadership team—including authors Mohammad Anwar, Frank Danna, Jeff Ma, Chris Pitre—vowed to bring humanity back to the workplace. Through trial, error, and determination, they rebuilt their organization around their greatest asset: people.

Today, through the Culture Rise experience and other products and services, Softway (www.softway.com) and Culture+ (www.culture-plus .com) are helping leaders worldwide transform their businesses by bringing humanity back to the workplace.

Index

217